SKOKIE PUBLIC LIBRARY
S0-ASN-327

Falling in Love Again

Marlene Dietrich

Falling in Love Again
Marlene Dietrich

DONALD SPOTO

Little, Brown and Company - Boston - Toronto

Other Books by Donald Spoto

THE KINDNESS OF STRANGERS:
The Life of Tennessee Williams

THE DARK SIDE OF GENIUS:
The Life of Alfred Hitchcock

CAMERADO:
Hollywood and the American Man

STANLEY KRAMER:
Film Maker

THE ART OF ALFRED HITCHCOCK

FIRST EDITION

LIBRARY OF CONGRESS CATALOGING IN PUBLICATION DATA

Spoto, Donald, 1941–
Falling in love again, Marlene Dietrich.

1. Dietrich, Marlene. I. Title.
PN2658.D5S6 1985 791.43'028'0924 85-15204
ISBN 0-316-80724-9

Published simultaneously in Canada
by Little, Brown & Company (Canada) Limited

PRINTED IN THE UNITED STATES OF AMERICA

for Elaine Markson
with grateful affection

Falling in love again,
Never wanted to —
What am I to do?
Can't help it!

The Blue Angel

CONTENTS

INTRODUCTION

WHEN MARLENE DIETRICH arrived in America in 1930, she was virtually unknown. Within weeks, however, she was in such demand to be photographed that appointments were made six months in advance. This book attempts to explore, in picture and word, the origins, the reasons and the means by which her powerful appeal has lasted for most of the twentieth century.

Some countries have royal families and a titled aristocracy, and those who support them emotionally and financially believe that a royal family embodies something finely representative of a nation's best traditions. In the United States, movie stars were for decades our nobility, and when the Great Depression spread bitterness and despair over much of the country, many in America looked to the silver screen to provide inexpensive encouragement and relief from the prevalent social gloom. Together in the darkness, people could behold Clark Gable as "The King," and soon there was John Wayne—"The Duke"—and more than one actress was called a "Movie Queen." Among a vast array of photographed stars, Marlene Dietrich, an immigrant, shone for decades with a luminous attraction that was often aristocratic, sometimes noble, but always beyond the rest of us poor mortals. It wasn't simply her veiled glance, her famous legs, that strange hint of a deeply knowing smile that fascinated. She was *there*—on the local screen—but she was certainly never fully comprehensible. She was, quite literally, alluring: she captivated, enticed, drew us on. But the visible charm—and the audible mystery in that slightly breathless, hesitant voice—left something undisclosed and remote. She was clearly a woman of flesh and blood and passion, but part of her seemed to have been transfigured, glorified—and not only by lights and lenses and mirrors. It was as if she had already stepped over the border into another realm of existence.

From the beginning of her career in America, there was something distinct and eloquent about Dietrich's presence amid the uncertainties of everyday life. She had a splendid face, haunting eyes and a famous figure, and her features were quietly exotic, with the hint of a confident, languid sexuality that was neither hysterical nor crude. As a German, trained on the Berlin stage and apprenticed in that country's postwar cinema, she brought a quality rare and articulate to our domestic audiences, who were accustomed to a series of brassy musicals, serious melodramas, talky photoplays and sappy crime or horror thrillers. Her place is assured because of a stunning variety of presences she could suggest—women of elegance, maturity, passion, innocence, resignation, simplicity or superiority—presences that, thanks to the motion and still pictures, endure to this day.

This book is simply structured, and nothing like a biography. In addition to films, Dietrich had a successful career in concert stage recitals, on radio and records and television, and as a documentary narrator. But it's difficult to appreciate performances for which there are no elucidating images, and so I've restricted myself to a consideration of her movies, and to conclude with her last substantial film performance, in *Judgment at Nuremberg*. Two brief screen appearances followed, but the first was a momentary cameo, and the second was (as she was the first to admit) most unfortunate: in 1978, frail but insistent, she played a bordello madame in David Hemmings's *Just a Gigolo,* which was set in Berlin at the end of World War I. She was, according to one friend, quite heartbroken after she'd done that.

Falling In Love Again is offered as a reflection on Marlene Dietrich's place in the developing awareness about Woman in our time. It's also intended as a grateful tribute to one woman's dignity, warmth and generous humanity—qualities which for me always triumphed over the distance, coolness or remoteness sometimes associated with her. To celebrate Marlene Dietrich is to honor her beauty and talent, to be sure. But it is also to honor our own capacity for wonder.

ONE: GERMANY

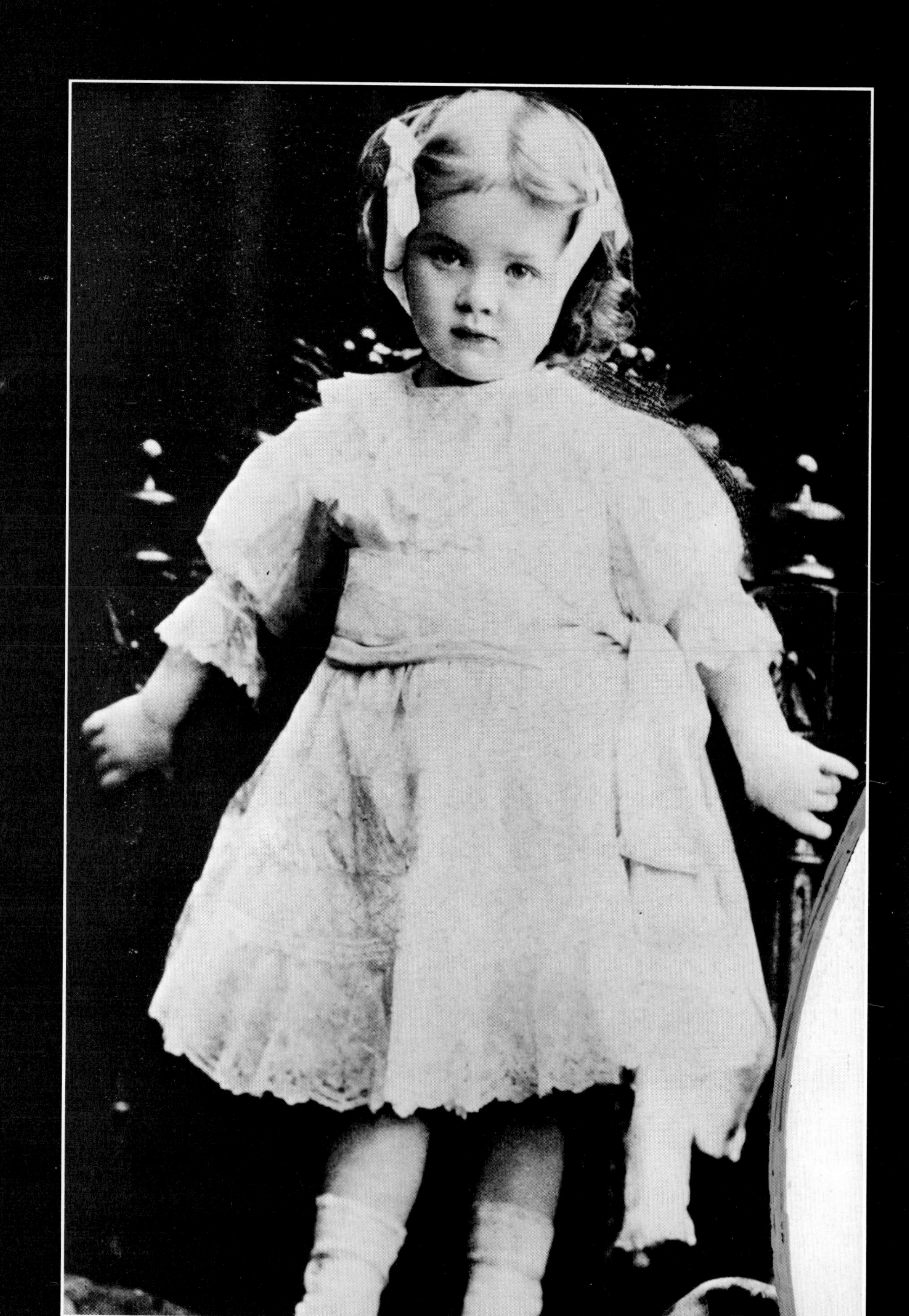

"AS A CHILD," according to Marlene Dietrich, "I was thin, pale, with long sandy hair; I had a translucent complexion, with the white skin common to redheads —and thus, because of the sandy hair, I had a sickly appearance." The few surviving photos of her reveal a child with long hair, but one not especially sickly in appearance. In fact, according to the fashion of German menus at the time, young Maria Magdalene Dietrich (so she was christened the day after her birth on December 27, 1901) was fed a generous diet, rich in carbohydrates and indulgent with sweets. By the time Maria Magdalene was ten, her sister Elisabeth (a year older) pointed out to her that she was, to put it bluntly, fat. This was perhaps the first example of a wide distance between her own memory and others' perceptions.

At age two, Maria Magdalene Dietrich, here at home in Berlin, had already the look of cool determination the camera would capture for decades . . .

Diet was not the only extravagance in Germany during the early years of this century. The country was experiencing astonishing prosperity, and as the German-American historian Richard Plant has noted, "There was monumental bad taste in every aspect of style—overstuffed Victorian draperies and furniture, sumptuous dinners, and everywhere an unchecked conspicuous consumption. Patriotic marches took on a vaudeville character. To sum it up, it was an age of gigantic *kitsch*."

The Dietrich home was no exception, and along with the typically Teutonic sense of duty there were abundant privileges and pleasures. German to the marrow of her bones, Wilhelmina Felsing Dietrich encouraged her daughters in the fine arts as well as the homemaking crafts. Her daughters remembered her as a woman of aristocratic bearing ("rather like a benevolent general,"

. . . and by the age of five, in spite of her mother's taste in hats, the little girl's innocence had an appealing, clear-eyed directness.

Marlene recalled), independent, stolid, sometimes even stoic. Her husband, Louis Erich Dietrich, was a professional army officer who had served with distinction in the Franco-Prussian War. He was so often absent on military training maneuvers that his wife and daughters had to rely on their own strengths, talents, emotional resources and wits to supplement their income for the requisite luxuries. It was, in other words, a woman's world: the nearest relatives were exclusively women, too, as were the local teachers and, of course, the household servants.

The family was not extravagantly rich, to be sure, but the Felsings had for decades traded in jewelry and timepieces, and Herr Dietrich's military salary—turned over each month to his wife—assured that the family could enjoy worriless comfort. That comfort was not interrupted by his death in 1911, for Frau Dietrich married another military man, Eduard von Losch.

In spite of the ancient antipathies between Germany and France, French language and culture were taught daily in the schools, and a young Frenchwoman named Marguerite Bréguand instilled in Maria Magdalene an appreciation of the Gallic tradition that endured long after the teacher was removed at the start of World War I. "The war brought an epidemic of patriotic madness," as Richard Plant remembered. "In our schools all we heard was *Gott straffe Frankreich:* 'May God punish France!' " This was an attitude Maria Magdalene could never appreciate, never endorse.

Until the war and its ugly interruption of the von Loschs' quietly privileged life, there were rich cultural and social advantages. Maria was taught both piano and violin, she regularly attended concerts, and she was taught the classics at home. Her mother also exposed her to Shakespeare, Sophocles and Mozart—as well as to poetry and opera—and Goethe became her "god," as she claims in her memoirs.

But the violin had pride of place in her life, and at least one music instructor was so enthusiastic that he told her mother there was a concert career ahead. When the family moved from central Berlin for a few years, a new teacher continued long practice sessions, endless Bach exercises that had an unfortunate result: a ligament in her left ring finger became severely inflamed, her hand was immobilized in a cast, and it was soon clear that any serious hope of a musical profession had ended. Her mother, to cheer her, gave her more to read—poetry in great quantities—especially Rilke's gently lugubrious lyrics and the *Sonnets to Orpheus.* By the time she was sixteen, she had decided on another public career—as a stage actress, "since the theater was the only place where you

7 / *Germany*

could recite great words and verses, like Rilke's," she wrote later.

The war impoverished very many in Germany—and disillusioned everyone—and the Dietrich/von Losch family was not exempt from misfortune. Marlene's stepfather was wounded on the Russian front, where he was visited by his wife; she returned to her daughters shaken but determined to endure whatever the outcome. Soon the news arrived: he had succumbed to infection. From this time, the household was an even quieter place, order and discipline and devotion to daily duties providing a kind of stance against the chaos that death had brought.

Maria's intense energies were unflagging, however, as was her ambition to succeed on the stage. Since childhood, her two names had been easily contracted to "Marlene," and with the name Marlene Dietrich she applied in 1921 to Max Reinhardt's famous acting school in Berlin. A former bank clerk and performer, Reinhardt (born Max Goldmann, near Vienna) had been since 1905 the director of the famed Deutsches Theater. His productions of Shakespeare and Sophocles were the same that had earlier inspired the young Marlene, and she had also seen his premiere production of Richard Strauss's opera *Der Rosenkavalier* as well as his stagings of the *Kammerspiele* or chamber plays he presented on smaller stages near the Deutsches Theater.

For her audition to Reinhardt's school, Marlene was asked to recite Marguerite's prayer from Goethe's *Faust*. Apparently this impressed the faculty enough to ensure her immediate acceptance, and although she insisted forever after that she had no special talents and was very raw indeed, she pitched herself into acting classes and scene preparations with the gay and passionate zeal of the young apprentice. "To be accepted by Reinhardt's faculty was virtually to be guaranteed acting jobs in Berlin," according to Richard Plant. Soon Dietrich could be seen in crowd scenes of the more lavish productions.

She had, like very many German women at that time, a somewhat ample, Rubenesque figure. But she could be prettily draped by a keen-eyed costume designer, and she was an attractive addition to the long lists of featured players. Sometimes she also had a line or two of dialogue.

From 1920 to 1923 the German economy was in a sudden and fierce decline, while inflation gradually ruined millions. A military pension was worth about ten dollars a month, and inheritances were almost without value. Social life became, as Plant remembered, "a wild, often desperate attempt to enjoy the passing moment, and cabaret life flourished as never before." Eager to help support her family, Marlene accepted every stage role without discretion or complaint — most of them, she claimed later, were forgettable; indeed, it is hard to find any evidence in the newspapers or review journals of anything notable in her career at this time.

But during that same period, the film studios were busy sending scouts to the streets, the schools and the theaters. For those satisfied with bit parts and a single day's work, there were jobs aplenty. When two assistants to the film director Georg Jacoby announced a casting call for a comedy, therefore, Marlene and several friends were first to appear for an interview. In late autumn 1922, she began several days' work on an unexceptional costume comedy, *Der kleine Napoleon/Napoleon's Younger Brother* (also called *Men Are Like That,* among other foreign release titles).

For her second film role — in *Tragödie der Liebe/Tragedy of Love* — director Joe May had signed the most famous German film actor of the day, Emil Jannings, as leading man in a story of sexual intrigue and murder. May sent his assistant, Rudolf Sieber, to cast supporting roles, and Dietrich was chosen for the very small but noticeable part of a judge's mistress. Her single long scene — reclining in bed, begging her lover's permission to attend Jannings's trial for murder — barely survives in an incomplete patched version. But frame enlargements of the scene reveal what May and Sieber found so interesting: the languid confidence, the cool insolence and the uncomplicated sensuality of a young woman so at ease with her appeal that she very nearly takes it for granted. Her scene was all the more impressive since it was, of course, a silent movie: glance and gesture had to supply the intonation. ("I was proud that [Sieber] picked me," Dietrich wrote years later, "proud that I was not too young, too innocent, too — everything that in fact I was.")

But Sieber had his eye on more than Dietrich's suitability for a small role. They began a very proper courtship (usually in her mother's parlor and never, she insisted, without a chaperone) and two years later, in the spring of 1924, they were quietly married. The following year, their only child, Maria — nicknamed Heidede — was born.

"In the 1920s," as Richard Plant remembered, "the theatre and the arts in general were hugely successful in Germany. In Berlin alone there were at least twenty-seven theatres — all booked with productions and filled to capacity with spectators — and everywhere there were new writers with new plays, new music and musicals, and new stage and film design. Rich bankers pro-

As a slightly doughy peasant girl in Der Mensch am Wege/Man by the Roadside *(1923), Marlene Dietrich's gaze was nearly provocative, although the director insisted that her character in the film was purity incarnate.*

vided whatever funds were not given by the state. It was the heyday of Kurt Weill, Bertolt Brecht, the Bauhaus—an unparalleled era of imagination, energy, excess, sometimes even genius."

At the same time, Marlene Dietrich's career kept a busy if somewhat monotonous pace. Friends and colleagues who knew her then insist that her real joy was her daughter, and that she worked at studios and rehearsal halls not one moment longer than her duty required. Always prompt and professional, she pursued her career for the income. Household help never lasted long at the Sieber address—not because Madame was difficult to please (although she could indeed be just that) but because she preferred to do the chores herself; the help, she felt, deprived her of her great pleasure.

This aspect of Marlene's personality always arouses amused incredulity, but the fact is indisputable. She did what she did in her career because it enabled her to support the two people she most loved; later, because it provided her with access to stimulating company and an independent life. She took acting seriously only insofar as she always wanted to be a dutiful worker; she rarely took the effect of her acting seriously at all—which is to say that she never saw her contributions as having the slightest cultural significance. The only thing to which she attached importance in the 1920s was cooking for Sieber and their daughter, or cleaning the house. "She's a cook first, a grandmother second and everything else thrown in for good measure," according to Maximilian Schell, who interviewed her when she was past eighty. Very little had changed in sixty years.

The films she appeared in during the early years were common variations on themes of love, sex, theft, guilt, death—the garden varieties of chancy melodramas that the culture devoured. In *Der Mensch am Wege/Man by the Roadside* she was a simple peasant girl; in *Der Sprung ins Leben/The Leap into Life* she flitted briefly across the screen as an extra; in G. W. Pabst's landmark treatment of postwar despair, *Die freudlose Gasse/The Street of Sorrow* (which starred Asta Nielsen and Greta Garbo), she was an unbilled extra again. Her professional boredom was not relieved by the films that followed: in *Manon Lescaut* she was a typical demimondaine, and she had a similar role in Alexander Korda's version of *Eine DuBarry von Heute/A Modern DuBarry.* For the latter she (or a sleepy technician) briefly altered her name in the credits—to "Marlaine."

She then took a tiny walk-on for Korda in *Madame wünscht keine Kinder/Madame Wants No Children* before playing a series of eligible charmers—in *Kopf hoch, Charly!/Heads Up, Charly!*

Dietrich's pale simplicity and languid distraction were, she later wrote, simply manifestations of her own boredom during the shooting of her silent films. In Eine DuBarry von Heute/A Modern DuBarry *(1926), she was credited as "Marlaine Dietrich."*

she was a Frenchwoman ripe for marriage, a role she repeated in *Der Juxbaron/The Imaginary Baron,* opposite the great Reinhold Schünzel. Another farce followed, in which she was more glamorously bedecked than ever, and in which her legs received even more exposure: in *Sein grösster Bluff/His Greatest Bluff* she was a call girl/thief capable of amorous deceptions. With almost harrowing monotony, she then accepted the role of another larcenous amoreuse, in *Wenn ein Weib den Weg verliert/Café Electric.* This led to her most daring role so far, as *Prinzessin Olala/Princess Olala* (as in oo-la-la!), a courtesan who gives men lessons in lovemaking and also encourages them with sisterly counsel—rather like an early Xaviera Hollander. The amusing glances she tossed at everyone else in the story, however, suggested to some critics that Miss Dietrich's onscreen contempt for the whole sordid business just might not be an act. Outside the studios, after all, she avoided publicity and hurried home (usually with an armful of groceries) to her husband and daughter.

An appealing comedy called *Ich küsse ihre Hand, Madame/I Kiss Your Hand, Madame*—released early in 1929—gave her a leading role, as a flirtatious Parisian divorcée. The object of every

In several early silents, Dietrich was turned into a vampish brunette; in Sein grösster Bluff/His Greatest Bluff *(1927) she was a larcenous call girl given to nonstop amorous deceptions. Harry Piel was her director and leading man.*

As a courtesan who gives lessons in lovemaking, Dietrich (here with Carmen Boni in Prinzessin Olala/Princess Olala, *1928) was rather like an early Xaviera Hollander, but with much more self-mockery.*

Harry Liedtke receives the equivalent of his walking papers from a coyly flirtatious Dietrich in the appealing 1929 comedy Ich küsse ihre Hand, Madame/I Kiss Your Hand, Madame . . .

. . . and in the same film, when her aptly named costar, Karl Huszar-Puffy, offered to do anything in the world for her, she replied with a straight face, "All right, you can take my dogs for a walk."

man's desire, she dispatches her overly attentive and obese lawyer who offers to do anything in the world for her: "All right," she replies with the merest elevation of her eyelids, "you can take my dogs for a walk."

By this time, most men in the movie theatres would have gladly walked dogs for her, for although she was not a major motion picture star she could regularly be seen and was known as a competent and attractive presence. Her films might have been uneven, repetitious in their tottering attempts to inject farce into sexual intrigue or German jazz-age cynicism into perfumed soap opera. But in film after film something was, perhaps unconsciously, emerging — not only a stability and a confidence, and not only the refracted maturity of a wife and mother and dutiful professional. The sharper lenses, the more varied focuses of the late 1920s cameras recorded something deeper, a mysterious perception, a kind of emotional distance from the frequent foolishness of the narratives. Sophisticated lighting techniques and lenses that blurred backgrounds and suffused foregrounds and actors with halos could not, after all, put expressions where they were not. It was indeed Dietrich's richly ambiguous gaze, her announcement that here was a *woman* — not someone identical with the part she played, and certainly never credible as anything like a

Depression-era European flapper. There were suggestions of a complex character behind her gaze. The veils added later by Josef von Sternberg really only italicized the admixtures of calm, of a wise awareness of human nature and of a sometimes maddening insouciance.

The novelist John Fowles has written of "visual things the word can never capture," and of "the appalling paucity of vocabulary to define the endless nuances of facial expression" of which we humans are capable. Dietrich never gave the impression of "endless nuances"— she was not the woman of a thousand faces. But she effectively demolished the bromides that if a woman is cool she can't be passionate, that if she's reserved she can't be forthright, that if she holds something back she's a tease.

While looking at the other players in her films, even those of the 1920s, Dietrich seemed to be looking at us. And what she communicated was a sense that adult life and emotions are a mysterious business, infinitely fascinating and never to be taken for granted. Certainly *she* would never be taken for granted. When audiences looked up at her on the screen, she didn't seem — then or later — to be looking down.

She died, for the first but not the last time on screen, in her next film, *Die Frau nach der Man sich sehnt/Three Loves.* As a *femme fatale* shot by a deranged lover, she expires gently, but a moment before the end she stirs — as if roused from a dream. "I have lost them all," she laments with an almost mystic calm, referring to the husband whose murder she abetted, to the lover whose embraces have become repellent, and to a young Frenchman she has lately met. A woman in constant pursuit of the one great love of her life, she knows at the last the impossibility of such an ideal. Death, therefore, is not entirely unwelcome.

Three Loves was an unusually frank film, with its brutally erotic wedding night and its exploration of emotional and sexual sadomasochism. This wasn't of the pathological bondage-and-discipline type that has become almost fashionable in some places today; it was the kind of sexual enslavement resulting from criminal collusion. Those who commit a crime in order to be "free for love" chain themselves in the worst bondage of all.

By the time the film was released Dietrich had completed her next, *Das Schiff der verlorenen Menschen/The Ship of Lost Men,* in which she played an American aviatrix whose plane crashes into the sea. She's rescued by a ship whose men are at once lost to an animal passion for her, and her second rescue is as nick-of-time as

In Die Frau nach der Man sich sehnt *(released in America as* Three Loves, *1929), Dietrich portrayed a woman in constant pursuit of the one great love of her life. Fritz Kortner wasn't it.*

Robin Irvine, wearing more makeup than his costar, comforts Dietrich — an aviatrix rescued by a shipful of lusty men — in Das Schiff der verlorenen Menschen/The Ship of Lost Men *(1929). Windblown and grimy, she was still luminous . . .*

. . . but in the same film the camera also showed that she was, before The Blue Angel, *rather plump in her clunky male attire.*

Her last film before international stardom was Gefahren der Brautzeit/Dangers of the Engagement Period *(1929), as a sweet girl seduced by a Casanova. The veil, the half-closed lids and the knowing smile suggested a deeper awareness, however. Willi Forst was the leading man.*

the first. The picture was notable for its beguiling use of darkness and grays (the director was the formidable Frenchman Maurice Tourneur) and for the revelation that a woman (or at least *this* woman) could, even in clunky male attire, cause fever among the beasts.

Never away from a film studio more than two weeks from 1926 to 1929, she appeared the latter year in *Gefahren der Brautzeit/Dangers of the Engagement Period,* as a sweet girl seduced by a modern Casanova; he discovers, too late, that she's his best friend's wife.

As if the demands of filmmaking were insufficient to engage her, Dietrich also continued to assume whatever stage roles came along, with the inevitable results: she stood before the cameras from dawn to late afternoon, then before audiences in the evening, giving new meaning to the word stamina. Her theatre career, even after Reinhardt, was quite unremarkable: "I was totally unknown," she readily admitted later, "nothing but a debutante, one

Her daughter, Maria, nicknamed Heidede, was the absolute center of Dietrich's life. Dated 1929, this still from a neighbor's album was for years a family favorite; Maria was four.

actress among a hundred others." Rummaging through news files confirms this, even though she appeared in a series of light comedies and musical revues — among them, the German production of George Abbott's *Broadway;* Eric Charell's *From Mouth to Mouth;* and Mischa Spoliansky's *It's In the Air.* (In the latter she and the French actress Margo Lion sang a faintly lesbian duet about the highly charged affection that unites two girlfriends who go shopping, only to discover as they do so that it's much more fun without men.)

In these revues she sang or danced or strode across the stage with a pleasing, muted sensuality. Cabaret audiences glimpsed more and more of her naked thighs, and her voice — cheery, but then a trifle high-pitched — tossed off love songs or comic ditties, as the material dictated. She was indeed (if not for long) "one actress among a hundred others."

But there were serious enterprises, too. Reinhardt's faculty had put her in small Shakespearean roles (in *The Taming of the Shrew* and *A Midsummer Night's Dream*), in German repertory *(The School of Uznach)* and in productions of Shaw's *Misalliance* and *Back to Methuselah.* At least once she appeared with the great Elisabeth Bergner: Dietrich sat with her back to the audience and delivered a single line — during a bridge-playing scene, in which she said, "I pass."

From the end of 1929, however, the name, face and figure of Marlene Dietrich would never again be half-hidden or ignored among the credits. During the summer, the Austro-American director Josef von Sternberg arrived in Berlin to cast and film his adaptation of Heinrich Mann's novel *Professor Unrat.*

Born in Vienna, transplanted at an early age to New York, then back to Vienna and back to America, von Sternberg had various jobs until he settled in Hollywood in 1924 and directed a number of intense, idiosyncratic, often iconoclastic motion pictures — *The Salvation Hunters, Underworld, The Last Command* and *The Docks of New York* among them. His work was characterized by a bold naturalism, a pitilessly realistic view of human perversity, and by a brilliant technique that emphasized the dramatic uses of light and shadow, or props and scrims and smoke. Until 1923 he was simply Jo Sternberg, but while working as assistant director on a now forgotten film, the director and star (impressed with the long and musical names of other European luminaries) elongated his name to the more colorful Josef von Sternberg — "in order not to disturb the euphonic array of names that distinguished this undistinguished work," he recorded with typical irony in his autobiography. The change of name occurred "without my knowledge and without consulting me."

So much may be true, but over the next several years von Sternberg certainly developed into the kind of man who could have effected such a name-change quite by his own inspiration. Brilliant and unpredictable, autocratic and secretive, he was fond of sporting riding boots and a turban but he was not merely eccentric. He was a man deeply aware of international cultures who saw psychological affinities everywhere. Artist, poet and controlled master-planner of visual effects, von Sternberg kept everyone off guard. By 1929, he had been so successful that creative control over most of the production was his, and producer Erich Pommer had arranged to have him come to Germany with Emil Jannings, who had also been working in Hollywood to great acclaim.

Jannings — large and lumbering, and with an ego to match his girth — had convinced von Sternberg and Pommer of the merits of Mann's 1905 novel, about a bourgeois high-school teacher named Rath who marries a woman of easy virtue named Rosa Froehlich. A singer with a child by a former lover, Rosa is the cause of Rath's downfall. He loses his teaching post because of his association with her, and he then avenges himself on a society he considers petty and moralistic by becoming a gambler and crooked politician, using the wife who has used him, until they are both destroyed.

Von Sternberg completed his script by autumn, and the transformation from the novel was enormous. Called *Der blaue Engel/The Blue Angel* (after the nightclub in which the woman sings), it bore everywhere the marks of the director's own particular concerns. Those who were co-credited with the scenario "had nothing to do with the text," according to von Sternberg — and indeed they seem to have provided only details of German slang or of Berlin geography. The songs by Frederick Hollander and Robert Liebmann, von Sternberg insisted, would carry this early sound film — really the *first* German talkie, he claimed. Soon "They Call Me Naughty Lola" and "Falling in Love Again" were heard round the world.

Filming, however, was delayed. Von Sternberg had his supporting players — Hans Albers, Kurt Gerron and Rosa Valetti — from popular stage and screen productions of the day. But the right exponent for the leading lady had eluded him, in spite of Pommer's and Jannings's insistence on either Trude Hesterberg or Lucie Mannheim. Mannheim was finally the front-runner. She was a singularly bright star in 1929 — a sensuous popular beauty every-

"They Call Me Naughty Lola," Dietrich sings early in The Blue Angel, *at a cabaret remarkable for its moral murkiness and chorines even plumper than the star.*

one at the Ufa studio agreed was just right. But not von Sternberg, who claimed he needed "other elements than sheer outward beauty. Mere beauty in a woman can be as dull as the dullest film, and that is the very quintessence of dullness." He had decided to call his singing little coquette Lola-Lola ("so named by me and inspired by Wedekind's 'Lulu' "), and he pored over photos of every actress working in Germany. No one could be favorably stenciled against the image in his mind, an image of natural eroticism and mindless charm, an image of a woman entirely capable, if unwittingly capable, of causing a man the utmost degradation.

The resolution to the casting dilemma occurred when von Sternberg went to see the musical revue *Two Neckties,* by Georg Kaiser and Mischa Spoliansky, and which starred Albers and Valetti. In the cast was Marlene Dietrich.

"Here was the face I had sought," von Sternberg wrote years later, "and so far as I could tell, a figure that did justice to it. Moreover, there was something else I had not sought, something that told me that my search was over. She leaned against the wings with a cold disdain for the buffoonery."

Pommer and Jannings objected to the choice, but von Sternberg insisted on interviewing Dietrich. She arrived for her appointment "a study in apathy," according to von Sternberg, "giving me the impression that she might at any moment bump into the furniture." Jannings and Pommer took one look at what von Sternberg called her "bovine listlessness" and again demanded Lucie Mannheim, but the director was adamant: unless he was given his choice, he'd board the next ship for America. It was clear Dietrich had claimed him even before she had the job, even before the test. Mannheim was out of the running. (She turned up six years later, a sleekly glamorous spy, enigmatic and finally dispatched with a knife in her back, in Hitchcock's *The 39 Steps*.)

To the preparation of Marlene Dietrich's screen test von Sternberg devoted himself with religious fervor. "He had only one idea in his head," she wrote years later, "to take me from the theatre and make me a movie actress, to become my Pygmalion."

Since she had first impressed him in a musical revue, Pygma-

In top hat, short skirt, peekaboo underwear and a black gash of garters, Dietrich's characterization made Lola-Lola victim and victimizer in the Depression-era Berlin subculture. "I was just cheeky," she wrote years later, adding perhaps ironically that she "didn't know anything about sex and eroticism in those days."

Intending to scold her for her bad influence on his students, the staid professor (Emil Jannings) visits Lola-Lola's dressing-room and is immediately jellified by her charms. Never did so gentle a love-pat arouse such a storm of repressed energy.

lion told Galatea to report for the test with rehearsed songs and an accompanist, but she was so convinced that the role of Lola-Lola had no congruence with her own personality that she hardly prepared at all. "When you're young and stupid, which often go together," she wrote later, "you're barely aware of exceptional people. I simply pointed out to him that I wasn't photogenic, and urged him to hire someone else."

Von Sternberg took her lack of preparation as a further challenge, however, and he paid more attention to the photography of his discovery than to the presentation of two songs. Since she was in fact "bovine," Dietrich came to the test with a dress that resembled nothing so much as a scout's tent. No matter, von Sternberg muttered to her, pounds would disappear once he had the lights properly arranged: "I pinned the dress to fit her somehow, and pouring lights on her until the alchemy was complete, proceeded with the test. She came to life and responded to my instructions with an ease that I had never before encountered. . . . Her remarkable vitality had been channeled." Within days, Pommer and Jannings capitulated, and Marlene Dietrich was en route to international stardom; her days as a local, quite ordinary film actress and cabaret performer were numbered.

To think that Lola-Lola can be a homey companion backstage is to court disaster, as Jannings discovers: he becomes her fall guy, an empty, ruined clown. But von Sternberg drew, in scenes like this, a sudden vague simplicity from Dietrich— and the character thus became more complex.

The filming of *The Blue Angel* lasted from November 1929 to early February 1930, and Dietrich found that von Sternberg had greatly altered the novel she had read several times just before first scenes were recorded. The scenario now emphasized the teacher's harsh and humorless moralism with his high-school students, the boys who trade postcards of the naughty Lola-Lola in top hat, short skirt, bare legs and a black gash of garters pointing to the forbidden realms above her thighs. Professor Rath (the title of the novel, *Professor Unrat,* puns on his name: *Unrat* is the German word for garbage, or even excrement) sets out to scold the shameless woman for her bad influence on the young, but after only one visit to her dressing room he is hopelessly demolished by her charms and his own long-repressed libido. He spends the night with her, proposes marriage and abandons his profession and social status by becoming a member of her troupe. Eventually he is so degraded by his own worst instincts that he becomes a patsy in the company's cheap vaudeville routines—even while his wife turns to others for love.

At the end, the company returns to the town where he once taught, and he becomes a local laughingstock. After a fit of jealousy in which he nearly strangles Lola-Lola, Rath wanders back to his old classroom. There he dies, clutching the desk that once meant dignity. At the fadeout, Lola-Lola straddles a chair onstage, defying the audience at the Blue Angel café — and us — to risk a similar fate.

Jannings was paid $200,000 for his performance, and Dietrich only $5,000 — but his inflated salary did not assuage his offscreen jealousy as he observed von Sternberg's attention to his new star, and as he rightly perceived that she was being groomed for international celebrity status. During the scene of the attempted strangulation, in fact, he very nearly succeeded, and the supporting players and members of the crew had to drag him away from a shaken Marlene.

"Ridiculous — sitting on that keg up there," she insisted years later. "I was just cheeky. We didn't know anything about sex and eroticism in those days. . . . I, the well-raised girl, reserved, from a good family — I had succeeded, without knowing it, in rendering a unique performance. . . . I have no idea how von Sternberg achieved this miracle. Genius, I guess!"

On his side, von Sternberg found her the ideal apprentice. "Her behavior on my stage was a marvel to behold. Her attention was riveted on me. . . . She behaved as if she were there as my servant, first one to notice that I was looking about for a pencil, first to rush for a chair when I wanted to sit down. Not the slightest resistance was offered to my domination of her performance. Rarely did I have to take a scene with her more than once."

The "domination" of her performance paid off, and the film to this day conveys an extravagant air of careless cruelty: the whole milieu, as historian Siegfried Kracauer wrote, is one of "loosened instincts."

It's worthwhile to look at the structure of this historic motion picture, for von Sternberg's attention to detail was not limited to Dietrich's glance and dress.

The film opens with the professor finding his caged bird dead: "No more singing" announces his housekeeper coolly — which is true only until Rath's wedding party, when for joy over Lola-Lola he crows like a demented rooster, a big bird who's been animated by his passion for his new singing chickadee. Just before the final crisis of madness later, the crowing becomes an uncontrollable mania. By that time, the troupe, Lola-Lola and the townsfolk are all clamoring for his crowing act, and they hear it with a vengeance.

But the director's structure is subtler still. The first time we see Jannings in his classroom, he is teaching Hamlet's speech from the perch of his desk. "To be or not to be," he announces, and they

The conclusion of The Blue Angel: *Dietrich's attitude suggested there was something she despised about the twilight world of furtive eroticism. "These men are more doomed than I," she might be thinking, "because they're enjoying all this."*

recite. This dilemma, too, receives its tragic resolution in the same place, where later he dies.

Then, in the third sequence of *The Blue Angel,* Dietrich makes her first appearance — but only after we first see her image, a photo of her dropped by a careless schoolboy. From this von Sternberg dissolves to a rehearsal at the Blue Angel, and we glimpse Dietrich gazing over the cramped cabaret as if in a trance of boredom. The second shot is the crude cartoon of a blue angel, floating perilously over the heads of the chorus girls. And then, in the third shot, we see those gartered legs, seductively apart, as they will be at the final shot.

At once Dietrich sings "They Call Me Naughty Lola," and we're notified about this raucous cabaret world, this demimonde and its bold doyenne. She's not impressed by any man's display, nor by whatever she arouses. She's plump, but she's surrounded by so many who are downright fat that we don't notice. What we most emphatically *do* notice is the world in which this woman sings: it's one-dimensional, but she's not. A flicker of something hidden, something undiscovered by her mates (perhaps even by herself) is seen behind those heavy, smoke-dazed lids.

The Blue Angel is suffused from start to finish with a decadent haze; everywhere there are Peeping Toms, underwear fetishists, men all too willing to risk life for love. And Lola, smart little strudel that she is, knows that the passion never approximates anything like love.

This was the film that established once and for all — for American audiences, at any rate — that there was more to Europe than great halls and great wars, royalty and art and exotic entertainments and bold new furniture designs. There was also a Depression-era subculture as rank as anything Hollywood could ever concoct.

The social and moral meanness is located, of course, in the person of Lola-Lola. Unlike the exponent of the American notion of sex — as in Clara Bow, for instance, the prototypical flapper who had and gave *It* with giggling abandon — Dietrich suggested that there was something dark and perilous, and something she really despised about this twilight world of semifurtive eroticism. Her gaze is not so much leering or seductive as it is detached: "These men are silly little boys," she might be thinking. Or: "They're more doomed than I am because they love it here." We don't know just *what* she might be thinking. She's earthy, to be sure, but there's a hard-earned *sagesse* behind the *savoir-faire.* In contrast to the other logy chorines she has a weary indifference, as

After a preview screening of The Blue Angel *in Berlin in 1929, Dietrich — vastly different from Lola-Lola — welcomed an admiring Charles Chaplin.*

if she's seen all this for centuries. She's the modern version of the medieval Eternal Woman — not unrealistically pure, but not a despicable tramp, either — victim as well as unwitting victimizer in this crazy new dying era.

Dietrich was von Sternberg's representation of an even more universal notion, however. With her we see just how deadly it is to pursue illusion. To believe that Lola-Lola can be a charming companion is to court disaster, as Jannings discovers. This is the point of the magician in the film, always indicating the attendant illusion as well as the crude insult. Jannings literally gets egg on his face in the magician's act — an image appropriate to what's happening backstage, where his wife is making love to the strong-man. "Look at you," the magician says to Jannings moments later, "you — a man of culture — all this, for . . . a woman!" What a woman, some might say — but Lola-Lola/Dietrich would smile at that, too.

The film ends with the famous "Falling in Love Again," which is not the best rendering of the first line: "From head to toe I'm turned on for love" would be closer. "Men cluster to me like moths around a flame, and if their wings burn I know I'm not to blame."

Marlene Dietrich attached no particular merit to her performance, nor to the film either, as the opening night screening approached. "Nor did she attach value to anything else so far as I could ascertain," von Sternberg reflected later, "with the exception of her baby daughter, a musical saw, and some recordings by a singer called Whispering Jack Smith. She was inclined to jeer at herself and others, though she was extremely loyal to friends (many of whom were not always loyal to her) and quick to feel pity. . . . She was frank and outspoken to a degree that some might have termed tactless. Her personality was one of extreme sophistication and of an almost childish simplicity."

The sophistication and the childish simplicity were just what von Sternberg wanted to stress. And those were the qualities he emphasized in cables to B. P. Schulberg, production chief at Paramount in Los Angeles. For reasons that remain unclear, Ufa Studios did not take up Dietrich's option after *The Blue Angel* — perhaps because Jannings threatened to leave them if she remained. Von Sternberg then informed Schulberg that he was departing Berlin with Dietrich's original screen test and some clips from *The Blue Angel.*

Before *The Blue Angel* opened, on March 31, 1930, at the Gloria Palace on the Kurfurstendamm, a contract (with options) for Marlene Dietrich had been negotiated — by Josef von Sternberg, in Hollywood — to make films with him there, based on stories and scripts to be chosen and created by Josef von Sternberg.

"He was my almighty god," Marlene Dietrich admitted years later. And so she must have felt, for immediately after the premiere of *The Blue Angel* she followed him to the United States.

TWO: HOLLYWOOD

IN 1924, Josef von Sternberg wrote a short story —"The Waxen Galatea"—which was published in *The Director,* a Los Angeles magazine, the following year. As a clue to this director himself, it's indispensable. A shy man falls in love with a wax dress shop mannequin. Each day he gazes rapturously at the inanimate figure in the window until at last he sees a living woman who is the embodiment of it. He follows her, but she meets another man and humiliates her silent devotee. Shattered, the silent adorer vows never again to love anything other than a lifeless mannequin.

The uncostumed, unmadeup and unvarnished truth: Marlene Dietrich in 1930, in a photo she valued for its simplicity.

Direct and unsubtle, the story is of course a modernization of the Pygmalion-Galatea legend, except that in von Sternberg's version the living incarnation of the goddess turns out to be a disappointment. The filmmaker also stressed the gloomy fate of the worshipful lover, doomed to entertain an idealized and unattainable love.

When he arrived at Paramount Studios to prepare for Dietrich's subsequent arrival and their first American film together, von Sternberg began (with writer Jules Furthman) to adapt the novel *Amy Jolly,* a trifle by Benno Vigny that Dietrich had given von Sternberg for shipboard reading. By the time she joined him in Los Angeles (in mid-April 1930), the scenario was well advanced and there were enthusiastic reports about the European premiere of *The Blue Angel*—which would not, as it happened, be seen in the United States until after the next film.

Without her husband or daughter, Dietrich settled as best she

At home in Hollywood (1930): Lola-Lola has improved her station somewhat; the sexual allure, however, is by now part of the publicity package.

could into California life, meeting with von Sternberg about wardrobe and makeup for what was now to be called *Morocco,* and working to perfect her English.

"She was subject to severe depressions, though these were balanced by periods of unbelievable vigor," von Sternberg remembered of that time. "To exhaust her was not possible; it was she who exhausted others, and with enthusiasms few were able to share. At times provoking because of her peculiar superstitions, she balanced this with uncommon good sense which approached scholarship. The theatre was in her blood. . . . Her reading consisted of Hamsun, Lagerlöf, Hofmannsthal and Hölderlin. She worshipped Rilke."

Morocco carried further von Sternberg's peculiar vision of Marlene Dietrich as a fateful and fated woman, bound to a code of love that may be exotic but is certainly, in its rare sense of integrity and accommodation, not unadmirable. As finally realized, the film tells of Dietrich, a nightclub singer (again) who arrives in Morocco and, although pursued by the rich and elegant Adolphe Menjou, is drawn to the younger, handsome womanizer Gary Cooper. When she realizes that Cooper is more devoted to the wandering life of the foreign legion (and the array of women that his life makes available to him), she accepts Menjou. But the news that Cooper may have been a casualty while on maneuvers throws her into distraction, and when Cooper returns unhurt, she must—although grateful for the devotion and support of Menjou—follow the legionnaire even into the desert. Certain to be hurt, she is bound to the honor of her own love for the man. Our last glimpse of her is a long shot as she slowly recedes against the horizon of an endlessly windswept desert. Her white chiffon dress and scarf blowing wildly, and the sirocco against her face, she doffs her shoes, hurrying to join the line of wanderers—men always on the move, and their women, consigned only to dream of an unattainable stability.

With Gary Cooper, in Morocco, *von Sternberg began to exploit the possibilities of adult sexual confusion: Dietrich was often the* apparently *more severe of the two, and Cooper was appropriately unsure of his attraction to this powerful woman.*

As filming began, Dietrich was anxious about her appearance — she had been, after all, a plump *Hausfrau* when you looked past the top hat of *The Blue Angel.* But as publicity photos early in the shooting indicated, she needn't have been concerned. Drastic measures had been taken after her arrival in Hollywood: she was ordered to lose thirty pounds, which she obediently shed at once; she was told that her face would be more mature, stronger, if several rear teeth were extracted, which they were — the bosses at Paramount were pleasantly surprised at the closer resemblance to MGM's Greta Garbo, and besides, the tooth-removal had worked for others, like Joan Crawford. Several minor adjustments were also made to her hairline, and to the front teeth. Over all these procedures von Sternberg hovered attentively. "He found me," Dietrich wrote later, "perfectly corresponding to the image he had given me . . . the image of a woman that von Sternberg wanted to realize on the screen wasn't scrawny and asexual, but full of life

"What am I bid for my apple, the fruit that made Adam so wise?"

In Morocco *(here, with Paul Porcasi), von Sternberg and Dietrich canonized the tradition of "La Garçonne," the boy/girl conundrum that Paris and Berlin found fascinating, and that a lesbian subculture in the 1920s occasionally glorified.*

and the sex-appeal of which Everyman dreams." The dreaming, of course, was first done by Josef von Sternberg himself.

Morocco opens with one of the longest and most impressive reverse tracking shots in film history. Lee Garmes, in the first of three films he photographed for von Sternberg, drew the camera from a closeup of an Arab and his recalcitrant donkey to an extreme long shot of an advancing band of legionnaires. The frame, from this shot, is then crowded with contrasting images of life and death, of commitment and betrayal: a smiling woman holds a death-skull over her head; a look of devotion is met with a smirk. The noisy opening panoply of the unmovable animal and the approaching army will be perfectly balanced by the concluding shots, of the retreating legion and the impatient Dietrich helping another woman drag a stubborn goat.

Dietrich's first appearance in the film must have drawn gasps from the American audience, for the resemblance to Greta Garbo is indeed uncanny. All in black, against the inkiest night, she steps out of the fog onboard the ship and is immediately noticed by Menjou. To his offer of assistance she replies "I won't need any help." We get her meaning: her type has ways of finding all kinds of help. But we see in her distracted weariness that she's sick of all this wandering.

Von Sternberg then moves the narrative to a crowded Moroccan café, where we find Dietrich as the main attraction. In white tie and tails and top hat, she's monumentally self-confident, apparently indifferent to the audience's initial rejection of her sexually ambivalent costume and attitude. Contemptuous of the rowdy spectators, she strolls along, smoking a cigarette and surveying the crowd (with much the same gaze as at the end of *The Blue Angel*). She rebuffs a man's crude pass, sings about the death of love, then moves toward an attractive woman. After the woman giggles nervously, Dietrich removes a flower from the woman's hair, then kisses her square on the lips. The flower, seconds later, is tossed to Cooper.

Then, in a short black outfit and a feather boa, Dietrich returns, making love to Cooper with her eyes and singing:

What am I bid for my apple,
The fruit that made Adam so wise?
On the historic night when he took a bite,
They discovered a new paradise.
An apple, they say, keeps the doctor away,
While his pretty young wife
Has the time of her life,
With the butcher, the baker, the candle-stick maker.
*Oh, what am I bid for my apple?**

Von Sternberg's camera, in *Morocco,* rarely moves toward or away from Dietrich—she's been so carefully lit, the effect is too perfect to allow for the more diffuse lighting of traveling shots. This has the odd effect of isolating her, of making her detached from her environment: to show us a closeup of Dietrich, von Sternberg has to cut—an entire new setup—thus effectively rendering her a person distant from others when she reacts. We're very close, in this regard, to the classic idea that style is content, that *how* the visual artist tells the story *is* itself the meaning. Manner, in other words, *is* matter. This woman, the camera tells us, inhabits a different continuum of time and space.

In those beguiling closeups, too, von Sternberg shows how aware he is of the erotic power of hair: the film is black and white, but somehow Dietrich seems to shimmer in a golden halo. "There's a foreign legion of women, too," she tells Cooper in one such moment, "but we have no uniforms, no flag, and no medals when we are brave—no wound stripes when we are hurt."

"Is there anything I can do to help you?" Cooper asks, repeating the opening scene's words uttered by Menjou.

"No—I've heard that before. Or do you think you can restore my faith in men?"

* "What Am I Bid For My Apple?" lyrics by Leo Robin.

Seconds before her pearls — and her life with Adolphe Menjou — break, Dietrich is about to dash away for news of Gary Cooper . . .

. . . whom she will follow even into the terror of the desert. The only sound is the dry, insistent legion drumbeats . . .

"Not me. Anybody who has faith in me is a sucker."

"You'd better go now," she says with quiet sadness. "I'm beginning to like you. I seem to have the unhappy faculty of causing trouble wherever I go. Every time a man has helped me there's been a price. What's yours?"

And with this first dialogue between them, the entire Dietrich/von Sternberg ethos is presented whole cloth. It's the lack of faith, the refusal to believe, the avoidance of commitment, that "cause trouble." It's the ceaseless wandering of her men, the terror of exclusivity, that wrecks their souls. "I changed my mind," Cooper says flatly—and with these words he leaves her. She's a *femme fatale,* all right, but *fatale* mostly for herself.

"Who are those women?" she later asks Menjou, pointing out the women who traipse after the legionnaires.

"I would call them the rear guard."

"How can they keep pace with the men?"

"Sometimes they catch up with them and sometimes they don't—and very often when they do they find their men dead."

"Those women must be mad."

"I don't know—you see, they love their men."

Menjou is, by now, the clear surrogate of von Sternberg himself, as Amy Jolly is his prismatic image of Dietrich. Like von Sternberg, Menjou is the protective mentor, calm on the outside but tragically, deeply in love. "You see," he tells his guests when she leaves him to follow Cooper, "I love her. I'll do anything to make her happy." (Moments before, Menjou said to Dietrich the

words von Sternberg may well have felt expressed his own feelings: "You want to thank me for bringing you here, for tonight, for these pearls. . . ." But he knows he doesn't really possess her, no matter how many pearls entwine her lovely neck.)

In the great final desert fadeout, von Sternberg conveyed how ruthlessly honest he was about romance. The scene is rendered without the synthetic sentiment a lush musical score would have provided; the only sound is the dry, insistent drumbeats receding. Dietrich gives up everything for her one great passion, even if it's hopeless, even if the last trek after Cooper and his legion is bound to mean more rejection, and an insufficient response.

. . . as she follows her man, her heart's desire. Bound to the honor of her love, she slowly recedes against the horizon of the windswept desert, her dress and scarf blowing wildly as she hurries to join the line of wanderers—men always on the move, and their women, consigned only to dream of an unattainable stability.

With Russian-born director Dimitri Buchowetzki and her husband Rudolf Sieber, at the Hollywood premiere of Morocco *(1930).*

"Never before had I met so beautiful a woman who had been so thoroughly discounted and undervalued," von Sternberg wrote tenderly of Dietrich. *Morocco* is an aesthetic giant-step beyond *The Blue Angel* (although few film archivists would agree) and it tempers its vision about loss and risk with a curious compassion, and a clear understanding about the likes of the ungrownup Cooper who — preternaturally handsome though he may be — will never be the man for the likes of Dietrich. Menjou may have been, but that's a one-sided perspective, claims the film.

Something more than role-confusion is announced when Dietrich appears in formal male attire in *Morocco.* "I had seen her wearing the full-dress regalia of a man, high hat and all, at a Berlin shindy, and so outfitted her [in *Morocco*]," von Sternberg claimed. "The formal male finery fitted her with much charm, and I not only wished to touch lightly on a lesbian accent . . . but also to demonstrate that her sensual appeal was not entirely due to the classic formation of her legs."

For her part, Dietrich, in one of her rare on-the-record statements about Rudolf Sieber (from whom she was separated geographically virtually forever after 1930, but whom she never divorced), admitted that it was he who first suggested she wear men's clothes and a monocle. Since 1900, she claimed, many cabaret singers cross-dressed for their acts. For her it began "when an actress named Vesta Tilly, then Ella Shields both wore men's clothes. And other English artists quickly imitated them. I wore that outfit because the best songs are written for men."

That explanation is fine so far as it goes, and it's a better one than that trousers are more comfortable — a reason she offered a few journalists for a year or two. But Dietrich knew very well that the tuxedo and the calculated, manly swagger were not costumes to support songs. They were part of the hallowed image of "La Garçonne," the boy/girl conundrum that Paris and Berlin found so fascinating in the 1920s, and that a lesbian subculture occasionally glorified. But it was so calmly and classily pitched that no one could accuse "Dietrich the Garçonne" of trying to seduce a woman. The outfit became part of the mysteriously unpredictable nature of this special woman. She defied categorization. Something essential about her was always unknowable.

Not very many critics knew (or seemed to care) about the shadings in Dietrich's screen image—that they were the work of von Sternberg. But there was no doubt, as the septet of their films continued, that a special symbiosis prevailed.

"I had seen her," Josef von Sternberg remembered, "wearing the full-dress regalia of a man, high hat and all, at a Berlin shindy, and so outfitted her [in Morocco*]. I wanted to demonstrate that her sensual appeal was not entirely due to the classic formation of her legs." But he also admitted that he wanted "to touch lightly [!] on a lesbian accent." Paramount's publicity department went along with the boldness.*

For her New York apartment in the 1930s, Dietrich's decorator was given free rein. The results very nearly reduced her to insignificance in publicity photos like this.

By the end of 1930, Paramount had had to engage a full-time staff, to handle Dietrich's fan mail, and she reserved several hours weekly to sign photographs. Von Sternberg commented that America's rich and famous wanted to be seen with her, and that before it became known that she was a wife and mother (a fact the studio took pains to conceal, the better to surround her in mystery), offers of marriage or concubinage abounded. "Dukes and generals and even the heads of nations wanted her to grace their tables," according to von Sternberg, who by this time was managing every aspect of Dietrich's professional and social life.

"How hard it must have been for him," she wrote in her memoirs years later. "I understood none of his aims and wishes, still less of the projects he was planning for his Trilby, his Eliza Doolittle, his Galatea — his dream of creating a woman according to his own ideal, like a painter makes a scene spring to life on a canvas. . . . I saw none of what he was doing. I detected none of his intentions. He had decided to make a star of me overnight, something to which I was indifferent. . . . I was young, vulnerable and there to charm the entire American public, but in my own eyes I remained what I always was: a German girl careful only to do her assigned duty, and nothing else. . . . He was a confessor, a critic, a master, a provider of all my needs, a counselor, a businessman, an impresario, a spokesman, the peacemaker of my life and home, my absolute patron. . . . He taught me thousands of things, as well as English and acting. God only knows if I really benefited from all this! I don't think I ever thanked him. But I do recall that he did not like signs of gratitude."

Before she returned to Germany for a holiday with her husband and daughter, Dietrich and von Sternberg finished a third film — once again, of his own invention. *Dishonored* tells the story of a streetwalker whose services are enlisted for espionage. Its real merit was to be the dizzy variety of costumes, coiffures, attitudes and styles Dietrich was encouraged to affect for the role. From a wild (and belabored) masked ball to a sequence as a border peasant, this Mata Hari is the coolest of spies — until, of course, she falls for an enemy (Victor McLaglen) and conspires in his escape. Convicted of treason, she walks to her execution in the elegant clothes she wore as a woman of the night, a "city escort." No one but von Sternberg could have pulled off the final moments: adjusting her veil in the reflection of a drawn sword-blade, she waits for the firing squad to do its work. But a young officer is torn with emotion over the imminent death of this beautiful woman. She wipes tears from his eyes with the blindfold offered to her, then takes advantage of a dreadful pause before the gunfire to check her

The real merit of Dishonored *(1931; with Warner Oland) was the dizzy variety of costumes, attitudes and styles for her role as a streetwalker turned patriotic spy. But once again, her gaze is worth five minutes of screen dialogue.*

If she was Paramount's answer to MGM's Greta Garbo, she had to be photographed like Garbo—which is what von Sternberg and cinematographer Lee Garmes managed for two or three shots in Dishonored . . .

. . . But in a similar outfit, with a change of lighting, Dietrich offered an ingenuous innocence rarely associated with Garbo . . .

makeup and to straighten her stockings—it's the reprise of the film's opening shot, the famous legs as a trademark. The insistent drumroll and the awful echo of the rifles have a chilling resonance (the scene was realized in an airplane hangar so von Sternberg could have the unprecedented tones and timbres of rifleshots, and the film won the Academy Award for sound). It's this kind of care, and the glorious insert shot of Dietrich's triumphant smile before the shots, that save the film from silliness.

Throughout, her slow, measured speech is part of a complete image, every phrase rhythmically timed by her director as much as the cadence of the shots. It's as if Dietrich were part icon from another world, part country nymph, part fallen angel and wholly the Woman of Eternity.

. . . Yet (also in Dishonored*) she could perform a man's espionage tasks without losing the mask of the enigmatic woman of mystery.*

The execution scene in Dishonored*: she's about to take the blindfold from the nervous young soldier, dry his tears with it, then adjust her makeup and straighten her stockings before the firing squad dispatches her. The scene triumphs precisely because of her cool, affectless gaze.*

The prototype of the "extended family": Rudolf and Marlene Dietrich Sieber, their daughter, Maria, and the ubiquitous Josef von Sternberg (1931).

Returning from her visit to her husband and daughter in Germany after completion of *Dishonored,* Dietrich was informed by von Sternberg that further films together would be dangerous for both of them. Her career would be inextricably linked with his, stymied by his complete control, and he would remain an ironic captive to her presence. That presence freed him from slavish fidelity to traditional film narrative and enabled him to create stunning images (sometimes for their own sake). But he must have felt, at the end of 1931, that there was a perilously proximate treadmill that might get them both nowhere after this.

Dietrich, however, was adamant. She could do nothing worthwhile without him, she insisted, and she told the executives at Paramount (who had to listen) that she would work with no other director. Von Sternberg got the order, and their next film together was *Shanghai Express.*

Neven more alluringly photographed — through an endless series of scrims, veils, smoky filters — Dietrich played the notorious Shanghai Lily, a woman of elegant disrepute (again!) who meets up with a former lover (Clive Brook) on the Chinese railroad. Based on a single page of a mediocre novel, the film carries forward the now almost hallowed Dietrich/von Sternberg persona: the tarnished woman (like Amy in *Morocco* and "X-27" in *Dishonored*) capable of deeper fidelity and higher morality than what people expect. (Von Sternberg, significantly, made Shanghai Lily's real name "Magdalen.") In a story reminiscent of *Tosca,* she agrees to the advances of a Chinese villain (Warner Oland, in a return appearance after a similar role in *Dishonored*) in order to save the man she's loved all along, through several years of separation and misunderstanding:

BROOK: I didn't think I'd ever run into you again, Magdalen.
DIETRICH: Have you thought much of me, Doc?
BROOK: How long has it been?
DIETRICH: Five years — almost.
BROOK: Well, for five years I've thought of nothing else, Magdalen.
DIETRICH: You were always polite, Doc. You haven't changed at all.
BROOK: You have, Magdalen — you've changed a lot.
DIETRICH: Have I lost my looks?
BROOK: No, you're more beautiful than ever.
DIETRICH: Well, how have I changed?
BROOK: I don't know — I wish I could describe it.
DIETRICH: Well, Doc, I've changed my name.
BROOK: Married?
DIETRICH: No. It took more than one man to change my name to Shanghai Lily.
BROOK: Shanghai Lily?
DIETRICH: Yes. The white flower of China. You've heard of me — and you've always believed what you've heard.
BROOK: I still do. Well, it was nice to see you again, Magdalen.
DIETRICH: Oh, I don't know.

On the basis of plot summary and dialogue excerpts, it would be easy to dismiss *Shanghai Express* as a typically sordid, unimaginatively romantic escapade set in a garishly exotic climate. In fact, however, von Sternberg surmounted the unhallowed clichés by a direct approach to his material. The new "Magdalen" is captured in a transcendent moment, alone in her compartment, as von Sternberg's camera moves toward her cool white hands, which slowly fold in a gesture of prayer. The shot is breathtaking because we're unaccustomed to thinking of Dietrich as a character whose

Her veils (especially in such profusion, in Shanghai Express, *1932) italicize the mystery — but they also invite effort, for behind the lines and stripes and bars and dots we glimpse eyes alert and serene, energetic, questioning, detached. Travis Banton's costumes totter on the brink of self-parody.*

As a woman of elegant disrepute (in Shanghai Express*), she conveys something beyond eros and passion; there's something about von Sternberg's Dietrich that's withheld, something our poor mortal vision can't get through to.*

The difference between eroticism and pornography in the cinema: here, Dietrich and Clive Brook (with help from the invisible von Sternberg) demonstrate the triumph of the erotic in adult sensibilities.

"When I needed your faith, you withheld it," she tells Brook. "Now when I don't need it and don't deserve it, you give it to me." Her moral complexity makes a character like Brook's trivial.

Capable of deeper fidelities than anyone expects, Dietrich in Shanghai Express *is willing to sacrifice herself for this impossibly chilly ex-lover. He's unfazed, she's momentarily terrified.*

concerns could be otherworldly; the shot is central to the film because it italicizes the essential mystery of the woman von Sternberg perceived in Marlene Dietrich — a woman whose past is transcended in some single moment of fidelity and wisdom in the present. Any human judgment, partial and prejudicial at best, is inadequate to describe the woman he shows us in these films.

"My apprenticeship in the arts," he wrote later, "began in a millinery shop. . . . I became familiar with the differences between Venetian lace and rose point, Alençon, Chantilly, Valenciennes, Brussels and Swiss. This painfully acquired knowledge may have bobbed up in my films." May, indeed: the lace and veils through which we see Dietrich in *Shanghai Express* (and, next, in *Blonde Venus*) are more than just sexy peekaboo. In his extreme attention to each angle of vision, each degree of clarity, von Sternberg implies that there's something of her that's always withheld, something our poor mortal vision can't get through to. "When I

"It took more than one man to change my name to Shanghai Lily."

needed your faith, you withheld it," she says to Brook. "Now when I don't need it and don't deserve it, you give it to me." But in the more mature world of von Sternberg, love is never a matter of a balance sheet, and needs and desserts rarely match up. The veils augur mystery; they also invite effort, for behind the lines and stripes and bars and dots we glimpse eyes alert and serene, full of energy, questions and detachment. Shanghai Lily, who has for several years thrown away her name and now risks her life because there can be nothing like love without her man (recall Cooper in *Morocco* and McLaglen in *Dishonored*), represents a perverse kind of triumph. In Dietrich's ambiguous configuration of this personality, we find something beyond sexual passion. In her Magdalen-infidelities we find a pilgrimage toward fidelity; her sacrifice for her lover is a greater gift than any man will ever appreciate. Perhaps the veil most of all, then, shields her features from the vulgarity of our prying, partial gaze.

But before she was Shanghai Lily, she was "Magdalen," and while she could pray with folded hands, Lily knew she'd be heard even with a cigarette . . .

. . . And once again, Paramount's publicity department took up von Sternberg's cue. In 1932, the almost mythic image became, with the simple addition of a cigarette, remarkably humanized.

Brilliant, autocratic and calculatedly eccentric, Josef von Sternberg affected the masculine equivalent of Dietrich's unearthly inner calm; here, he's at home, about 1932.

Von Sternberg insisted that he was "no enthusiast" of Dietrich, "but a cold-eyed mechanic critical of every movement. If there was any flattery, it was concentrated in a 'That's fine, it will do.' More often she listened to 'Turn your shoulders away from me and straighten out. . . . Drop your voice an octave and don't lisp. . . . Count to six and look at that lamp as if you could no longer live without it. . . . Stand where you are and don't move; the lights are being adjusted.' " And so it went, while the Eternal Woman temporized. No viewer of *Shanghai Express,* however, can doubt that this businesslike attitude on the set was counterpoised by feelings tenderer and far deeper in the quiet places of his heart.

Forward they and Paramount went, with a film genre uncongenial for both but all the rage in 1932. *Blonde Venus* was planned as a soap opera, to demonstrate that the coolly elegant sensuality of Dietrich could—again, Paramount insisted, just like MGM's Garbo—be slightly modulated for the story of a woman's rise and fall and rise again. At the height of the Depression, and with the Motion Picture Production Code not yet formulated, the vagaries of female virtue could be charted, and adultery could go unpunished. In other words, some of the cloudy complexity of real adult life could be described in movies without an archly corrective moralism.

The story is radio melodrama. Herbert Marshall, a scientist poisoned by his own radiation experiments, must go to Germany for a cure. His wife, Dietrich, returns to her stage career to earn the necessary money for his trip, and very soon after her husband's departure she becomes mistress to a rich, dashing but crooked politician—Cary Grant, of all people, then on the brink of stardom. Marshall returns, threatens to take their little boy (Dickie Moore) from her, and tosses her out. With that, she takes the child and begins a long and unhappy flight from husband and police. Finally she's caught, the son is handed over to Marshall, and Dietrich is sent away as an unfit mother and wife. In a triumph of indomitable Teutonic brio, however, she goes even further with her resumed cabaret career, and in Paris, she meets up again with Grant, who accompanies her home. There's a swift and unconvincing reunion with husband and son, Grant gracefully withdraws, and Dietrich's mother love revives—and with it, all of the temporal punishment due to sin is absolved.

We'll never know how clear the film's autobiographical network was intended in *Blonde Venus,* but it's certainly there—rather as if von Sternberg had been thinking of himself and his star

But as von Sternberg readily admitted, he could not give her what she did not have—an astonishing variety, as these contemporaneous poses reveal. She could suggest the unsmug but wise look of an amused, modern woman . . .

. . . or the uncomplicated sincerity of an innocent . . .

. . . or the languid, bold sexuality of someone you never treat lightly.

But what she could never make convincing was in fact her favorite real-life role—housewife and mother. In von Sternberg's Blonde Venus, *the* Hausfrau *scenes are beyond credibility, and even she seems about to laugh.*

"Taxi Belle Hooper" (Rita La Roy) tells housewife-turned-cabaret-star Dietrich (in Blonde Venus*) that she's called "Taxi, for short." And Dietrich asks, "Do you charge for the first mile?" To which La Roy snaps, "Say, are you trying to ride me?" And so on.*

as he tried to avoid the inevitable flaws in his script. Grant seems to be another von Sternberg surrogate, enchanted with Dietrich the first time he sees her perform in a musical revue. Marshall, as the husband, is a variant of Sieber, away in Germany while his wife pursues other theatrical interests in America. And the tiny tot is an easy substitute for Dietrich's own little girl.

All this could be dismissed as too neat, too schematic, except that about this time Mrs. Josef von Sternberg sued Dietrich for alienation of her husband's affection; the suit was challenged by Dietrich, and Mrs. von Sternberg recanted. Sieber arrived from Germany and took his place by his wife's side, and not long after, a kidnapping threat was made against their daughter. The result of all this was a severe anxiety *à trois* (or *à quatre* or *cinq*), which von Sternberg defused by transforming the whole real-life period during which *Blonde Venus* was prepared and produced. The project became sort of work-therapy.

The finished film as we have it is alternately parodic and gently amusing, touching, beguiling and impossible—the kind of hodgepodge that resulted from its creators' own confusions. But in every frame it's a von Sternberg land of smiles and American hallucinations, of backwater dreams and fantasies. Never convincing in the scenes as a devoted *Hausfrau* (which was, after all, her favorite real-life role), Dietrich's flickering, ironic smile could barely be suppressed in the picture—especially when von Sternberg seemed to interweave lines of dialogue that poked fun at the story itself. (One delicious scene introduces Dietrich to a prospective manager, and she's forced to stroll about and show her poise for him just as Dietrich had for Jannings and Pommer, in von Sternberg's presence, three years before in Berlin.) Soon Dietrich is at a nightspot, sparring with another performer (Rita La Roy), a girl who refuses to walk or take public transportation and is thus called Taxi Belle Hooper: "Taxi, for short," she snaps.

DIETRICH: Do you charge for the first mile?
LA ROY: Say, are you trying to ride me?

And so forth. This sort of thing gets a bit thick halfway through the film, but von Sternberg alters mood so swiftly we haven't time to be annoyed.

For most of *Blonde Venus,* Dietrich weaves in and out of aqueous shadows like a voluptuous mermaid, applying makeup with airy hauteur and defying custom and chance. In the justly famous "Hot Voodoo" sequence, however, von Sternberg risked everything—and won. Dietrich, attended by a line of blackface chorines, slowly emerges from a gorilla costume, drawing off the

Stepping from a gorilla costume, Dietrich becomes the blonde Venus of her nightclub: "Hot voodoo, I'm aflame, I'm really not to blame: that African tempo is meaner than mean! . . . I'm going to blazes—I want to be bad!" This is perhaps von Sternberg's new high (or low) in self-parodied silliness.

huge, hairy arms and replacing the ugly ape's head with a crude blond "Afro" wig. Then, smiling that benevolently contemptuous smile of amusement at the sheer vulgarity of it all, she sings as the camera moves slowly toward and away from her (she never budges from the careful arrangement of the preset lights on her):

Did you ever happen to hear of voodoo?
Hear it and you won't give a darn what you do!
Tomtoms put me under a cult of voodoo,
And the whole night long I don't know the right from wrong.
Hot voodoo, black as mud, hot voodoo in my blood—
That African tempo has made me a slave!
Hot voodoo, dance of sin, hot voodoo, worse than gin—
I'd follow a caveman right into his cave!
That beat gives me a wicked sensation,
My conscience wants to take a vacation.
Got voodoo head to toes, hot voodoo's burned my clothes—

I want to start dancing just wearing a smile!
Hot voodoo, I'm aflame, I'm really not to blame:
That African tempo is meaner than mean.
Hot voodoo makes me brave, I want to misbehave,
I'm beginning to feel like an African queen!
Those drums bring out the devil inside me,
I need some great big angel to guide me.
Hot voodoo gets me wild—oh, fireman, save this child!
*I'm going to blazes—I want to be bad!**

And with that, Cary Grant is hooked, even as we wipe tears of laughter.

From this point, the story itself is designed to evoke an odd mixture of laughter and tears, as we follow Dietrich on a descent to the twilight world of the demimondaine: the theme of degradation for the sake of love was never so turgidly rendered by the director, and it's impossible to take seriously that cheeky little Dickie Moore, who strikes points for Planned Parenthood. It's worth remarking, nevertheless, that the director—heedless of an emotionally unbalanced narrative—was at the same time most attentive to lighting his Galatea. Key-lighting had been almost an obsession in *Shanghai Express.* "The light source used for closeups," Dietrich wrote later, "in my case created a face. . . . The mysterious-looking face with hollow cheeks [in *Shanghai Express*] was effected by putting the key light near the face and very high over it." Now, for his blonde Venus, back lighting was used. Again, Dietrich's description:

"Back lighting became very much the style . . . but it had its drawbacks. The cameraman always used to insist that your head not be moved to the side, since the light—placed behind you—then fell on your nose, which at once looked like W. C. Fields's. And so most scenes played opposite a partner were, to say the least, extremely stilted. We addressed each other while looking at some fixed point in front of us instead of looking into the other's eyes. It was the same for love scenes. We all had a marvelous allure in the halo of back lighting, but we stood straight as posts."

This is exactly the visual texture of the song scenes in *Blonde Venus,* and von Sternberg made a virtue of necessity again, demanding lyrics from Sam Coslow for Ralph Rainger's second song for her—lyrics for which von Sternberg could effectively and dramatically light her. For "Hot Voodoo," she had scarcely moved; for "You Little So-and-So," von Sternberg made certain she'd move, and that her words would enable her to do so with a meringue-light charm. In a single, fluid tracking shot, von Sternberg took Dietrich from a cabaret curtain, along rows of specta-

* "Hot Voodoo" lyrics by Sam Coslow.

But von Sternberg still knew how to pour dreamlike lighting on two handsome presences; here, Dietrich and Cary Grant in an inexplicably brief scene indicating they're having an affair — and, apparently, that they're equestrians.

*A benighted mother, on the run from the police? Only adorable little Dickie Moore knows for sure (*Blonde Venus*, 1932). The film, alas, very nearly drowned in its own suds.*

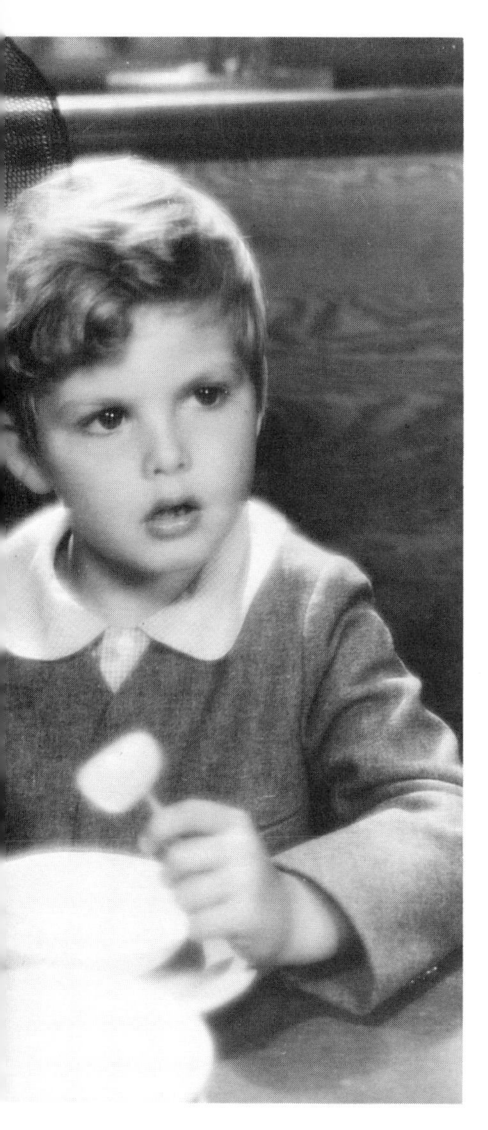

In a single, fluid tracking shot, as she sings "You Little So-and-So" in Blonde Venus, *von Sternberg took Dietrich from a cabaret curtain, along rows of spectators and then back again, photographing her through potted palms, gauze curtains and filtered lights, and over heads of spectators. For the studio still photographer, she paused before this impressive shot began.*

Tracked down by a private detective (Sidney Toler), Dietrich was dressed to suggest an unfit mother, but designer Travis Banton and von Sternberg finally presented nothing so much as Early Thrift Shop (Blonde Venus).

tors and then back again, photographing her through potted palms, gauze curtains and filtered lights, and over heads of spectators as she smilingly sings:

It isn't often that I want a man,
But when I do it's just too bad.
I know you're acting hard to get and yet,
I have the feeling you can be had!
You so-and-so, you little so-and-so,
Look what you've done to me!
You're almost twice as bad as (Who's this again?)
I ought to take you out and (Where have you been?) . . .
You this-and-that, you've got me you-know-what,
Is that the way to be?
The Greeks have words for almost everything I know
But: "you little so-and-so."
You so-and-so, you little so-and-so:
How did you get that way?
Although you know that I have lost my control,
You sit and talk about my beautiful soul.
You this-and-that, you've got me you-know-what,
Is that the way to be?
The Greeks have words for almost everything I know
But: "you little so-and-so!"

The most compelling scene in Blonde Venus *is set at a woman's shelter, where Dietrich, as a drunken castaway, raves that (by heaven!) she ain't done yet, and that she'll save herself. In spite of the overwritten clichés, Dietrich is extraordinarily convincing, sort of a chilling Madonna* manquée.

. . . And at once von Sternberg cuts to Paris, where the blonde Venus is the toast of the town as she sings "I Wouldn't Be Annoyed." And who should turn up in the audience but Cary Grant, who takes her back home . . .

. . . for a reconciliation scene with husband Herbert Marshall.

Whereas the songs allowed Dietrich her deliciously ironic gaze and semidetached invitations, the spoken dialogue did not allow her much range at all — except for one compelling scene in which, as a drunken castaway, she raves, at a woman's shelter, that by heaven she ain't done yet, and that she'll save herself. Her performance is so deeply felt in this overwritten scene that we believe it when von Sternberg cuts to the next episode: she's become the toast of Paris, singing "I Wouldn't Be Annoyed" and not at all surprised to meet Cary Grant.

Throughout the 1930s, Dietrich was much sought after by international stars, for her company and her counsel. Suzy Vernon and Imperio Argentina were among the émigrés happy to be recorded in her retinue, although pictures like this occasionally set a few gossips to their task.

Paramount, the public and the critics watched von Sternberg and Dietrich very nearly slip and drown in the suds of *Blonde Venus,* and soon there was pressure for her to work with another director. The Russian-Armenian Rouben Mamoulian got the assignment: he had created the brilliant camera and lighting effects for *Applause* (1929) and *City Streets* (1931), and there was a big noise about the two films he produced and directed in 1932, *Dr. Jekyll and Mr. Hyde* and *Love Me Tonight.* The project chosen for the new collaboration was Herman Sudermann's 1908 novel of a sympathetic girl's moral and social decline—*Song of Songs*—in which, curiously enough, von Sternberg's Pygmalion-Galatea theme was never so clearly presented.

As a simple girl from the provinces, Dietrich moves to the city following the death of her father; once there, she takes refuge from an impossible aunt in the studio of a sculptor (Brian Aherne). Soon she's posing nude as his Galatea (Dietrich did pose nude, off-camera, for the charming statue we see in the film). Then she becomes the sculptor's mistress—and from there, when she's married off by her aunt to a baron (Lionel Atwill), it's a short ride to marital misery, accidental infidelity and social disgrace before a last-minute happy ending with the sculptor.

An impossible story was redeemed by Mamoulian's solid direction of a fresh, relaxed, mature Dietrich. Sometimes she was photographed in *Song of Songs* too beautifully, as too calmly enticing, too luminous to be credible. And she's not helped by having to recite dialogue from the *Blonde Venus* tradition of absurdity: "You forget—I'm a baroness. I have money, position, jewels, servants. I play the piano and speak French. I have everything a woman could want!" Sure.

Mamoulian, however, wanted to demonstrate to Paramount that he and Dietrich could together concoct believable emotion, and so he worked and drove her for one astonishingly moving scene. As she recites the Bible's Song of Solomon, with its elegantly turned phrases about the visit of a lover and the wholeness of pure human desire, Dietrich's voice arcs from longing to wonder to a sense of loss and abandonment: she's thinking of the contrast between the words and her experience. Then she sobs, her voice breaking in waves of sorrow, for she's an unfulfilled woman who has lost everything for an impossible love. (It's all yet another variant on Amy Jolly, "X-27," Shanghai Lily and the blonde Venus.) Mamoulian showed this scene to Greta Garbo when, several months later, he prepared her for *Queen Christina.* Typically, Garbo's reaction was not recorded.

In Song of Songs *(1933) Dietrich made her first American film with a director other than von Sternberg. Rouben Mamoulian guided her through the somewhat turgid melodramatics of a peasant girl who takes her piety to the city, where the predictable reversals occur.*

Before a forced marriage to a baron (Lionel Atwill), the girl of Song of Songs *posed nude as a sculptor's Galatea. And in fact, Marlene Dietrich herself posed nude for the film's statue.*

For Song of Songs, *director Rouben Mamoulian simplified Dietrich's elegance, made her beauty recognizably human, less extravagantly exotic than von Sternberg's presentation of her had been. Lionel Atwill (center) before the final fadeout, loses her to the considerably more dashing Brian Aherne.*

With Brian Aherne in Song of Songs. *Dietrich, at her most regally elegant, never seemed stuffy or morose; there was always a hint of sexual availability.*

At home in Hollywood, at the time of Song of Songs . . .

. . . *and costumed as the heroine of the film, at the door to her studio bungalow.*

In Song of Songs, *director Rouben Mamoulian drew a fresh, spontaneous appearance from Dietrich — an attitude hitherto latent during the von Sternberg pictures. Here, they discuss a scene . . .*

. . . and from her reaction moments later, there seems to have been cordial agreement. In fact, Dietrich was more relaxed during the production of this film than she'd felt in years.

During production of Song of Songs, *aviatrix Amelia Earhart visited the star. Four years later, Earhart's plane disappeared over the South Pacific Ocean.*

Running the gamut of autograph hounds at the Hollywood premiere of Song of Songs. *Brian Aherne is at extreme left.*

Throughout the production of The Scarlet Empress, *von Sternberg was confident. "Every detail," he wrote, "the scenery, the paintings, sculptures, costumes, story, photography, every gesture was dominated by me." The finished film is quite a guide to his swollen fantasies.*

The collaboration with Mamoulian had been effective, but when von Sternberg described to Paramount's executives his plans for a lavish spectacle, with Dietrich as Catherine the Great of Russia, the studio reunited the pair. The publicity department announced to the press that this would definitely be the last time von Sternberg and Dietrich would work together, but the news elicited the same reaction as a diva's "farewell recital"—there might be twenty a year, for how many years no one could guess. *The Scarlet Empress,* von Sternberg's self-described "excursion into style . . . [with] every detail, scenery, paintings, sculptures, costumes, story, photography, every gesture . . . dominated by me," quickly took shape as one of the most obsessive motion pictures ever designed or produced.

No matter that it merely suggests accuracy in the story of the young Catherine's transformation from Prussian maiden to powerful queen. In this film, von Sternberg entered deeply into the world of nightmare. With enormous grotesque, Gothic-expressionist figures dominating the action, with a fascination for barbaric tortures and psychological cruelties, with its florid, exaggerated costumes and swollen production values, *The Scarlet Empress* is either (depending on your view of von Sternberg's career at this stage) a bold experiment or the hyperbolic achievement of a director out of control. Amid oversize palace corridors and door-handles twelve feet off the ground, surrounded by vast figures of brooding icons, encircled by sycophants with accents more suitable for Brooklyn or Chicago, clothed in ermine, white fox, sable, almost suffocated in fog and smoke — out of this savage miasma of visual excess, Dietrich had only to stride or smile or peer down at her pathetic husband (Sam Jaffe) or her slightly furry lover (John Lodge).

The Scarlet Empress remains an oddity. Partly inspired by German expressionism's free use of distorted perspective to suggest mental derangement, it totters so often on the brink of satire that even a careful and appreciative viewer may be unsure of the appropriate responses to each scene. The film was, in any case, a colossal financial and critical failure — everyone cried "Enough!" even while von Sternberg was working, with Paramount's reluctant approval, on the last film for which they had contracted him, and the one which would indeed be his last with Dietrich. There was, quite simply, no place further to go, no visual effect, no exoticism left untried.

Von Sternberg wanted to call his film, based on a story by Pierre Louÿs, *Capriccio Espagnol;* Paramount, however, thought that too literary and impossible for audiences to pronounce. They

Dietrich's daughter, nine-year-old Maria Sieber, played the young Catherine the Great in early scenes of The Scarlet Empress . . .

. . . but a photo circulated by the studio at the same time showed an oddly perplexed little girl.

The Scarlet Empress *was von Sternberg's relentless excursion into style, with barely a nod to the historical accuracy of Catherine's transformation from Prussian maiden to powerful regent. Dietrich was ordinarily juxtaposed, as here, with some kind of expressionistic grotesquerie . . .*

. . . and frequently she was simply dwarfed by the film's vivid excesses. Her smile (when we can find it amid the savage miasma von Sternberg created) is like a clarifying benediction on all the weird hyperbole.

Dietrich's somewhat furry lover in The Scarlet Empress *was John Lodge, later a congressman, Connecticut governor, and ambassador to Spain and to Argentina— positions more congenial than that to which Hollywood and von Sternberg subjected him.*

Not even Dietrich's faintly satiric moments could save The Scarlet Empress. *Although it left no exoticism untried, it was a colossal critical and financial failure; in it, von Sternberg became a kind of victim to the very Dietrich myth he had created. A diaphanous idol had short-circuited his creative life.*

Constantly surrounded by vast, brooding icons and macabre figures of doubtful symbolic function, clothed in furs and pursued by John Lodge as Count Alexei, Dietrich's Catherine thus becomes prey to von Sternberg's excess of style . . .

. . . which extended to Travis Banton's military uniforms . . .

. . . and to an exaggeration of lines, material and sheer volume that more than once overstepped the boundary to satire.

It's not hard to imagine, therefore, that Dietrich was at least partly motivated, when she stepped out on her own, by a desire to be free of so much wardrobe impedimenta. *More often than not, her appearances in public were a brilliant combination of her preference for the casual and the bold.*

gave it the unfortunate final release title *The Devil Is a Woman.*

Set in 1890 Spain, it is a dizzy panoply of confetti, parades and ultrachic costumes. Virtually a résumé of the von Sternberg/Dietrich movies, the film stars her as the former lover to Lionel Atwill (shades of *Song of Songs*) who arouses the interest of Atwill's young friend Cesar Romero. Atwill allows himself to be wounded in a duel with Romero, since he believes Dietrich has put Romero in place of whatever feelings she may have had for himself. She then flees with Romero for a new life. But in a sudden reversal, she turns out to be no devil after all: at the end she leaves Romero, to return to the wounded Atwill and to a subsequent change of heart.

It's hard to know how to take this pudding of a narrative, unless we yield to the fascinating temptation to see it as a last stencil of the relationship between the director and his leading lady. Both Atwill and Romero bear striking resemblance to von Sternberg, and after the several attempts von Sternberg had made to sever their relationship (like Atwill himself in the long flashback), he found himself more emotionally linked to her than ever, and the final moments of *The Devil Is a Woman* suggest an awareness that, with dogged persistence, Dietrich remains with the one to whom she gave herself unreservedly (i.e., Atwill/von Sternberg).

However we see the picture, the visual texture is almost as excessive as that of *The Scarlet Empress,* without a surfeit of statues. Travis Banton's costumes for Dietrich were ludicrous overstatements of Spanish Traditional and 1935 High Fashion; it's doubtful they could have been worn by anyone other than Dietrich without being mistaken for Halloween outfits.

"The collaboration between von Sternberg and Travis Banton reached its zenith in the costumes for *The Devil Is a Woman,*" she wrote years later, "which is my favorite film and the most beautiful one ever made. Von Sternberg reserved the right to accept or reject what Travis and I had designed, always subject to his instructions. We worked during lunch, between takes and late into the night. Travis and I knew no fatigue, perhaps because we adored von Sternberg."

The filming, however, was a stormy experience, most of all because the director announced daily that his work with Miss Dietrich was complete with this film. "My being with her any further will not help her or me," he insisted. And in spite of her angry demands, her tearful pleas and her professionalism during production, Dietrich was finally resigned:

"When Josef von Sternberg decided to end our collaboration—aided and abetted, no doubt, by studio heads—a long series of

But she could, of course, also be one of the girls—as here, at a Hollywood premiere with Rouben Mamoulian, in 1934.

Rudolf Sieber and Josef von Sternberg with Marlene and Maria at a Los Angeles polo match, August 1934. At left is Tamara Matul, then identified as Dietrich's secretary. Later, she was Sieber's companion until his death in 1976, and, as her glance here suggests, she never welcomed publicity.

mediocre films began for me. . . . Before he took me in hand, I was totally unaware, I was no one, and the mysterious powers of this creator breathed life into this nothing. . . . I was only an obedient tool in the infinitely rich palette of his ideas and images. The films von Sternberg made with me speak for themselves. Nothing today or to come could surpass them. Filmmakers are forever doomed to imitate them."

Her first choice after completing the film was to leave movie acting altogether. "'If you leave Hollywood now,' he told me, 'everyone will think that I forced you to. You must continue to work here.' So I made the next films, without any conviction." Almost at once, in their public and private utterances, von Sternberg and Dietrich let it be known that something had died in their confidence in each other and their abilities—and for von Sternberg a professional decline began; during the next thirty-five years of his life, he completed only seven feature films, none of them widely popular.

Her last film with von Sternberg was The Devil Is a Woman, *a film almost as bad as its title implies. Travis Banton's wardrobe for her was a lush pudding of Spanish Traditional and 1935 High Fashion. We're very close, here, to what would later be called "camp."*

Lionel Atwill bears a striking resemblance to von Sternberg in The Devil Is a Woman; *in fact the key to the strange narrative may be the history of the director/star relationship.*

Dietrich moves from Atwill to Cesar Romero in The Devil Is a Woman, *which might have been subtitled* Experiment in Fashion, 1935 . . .

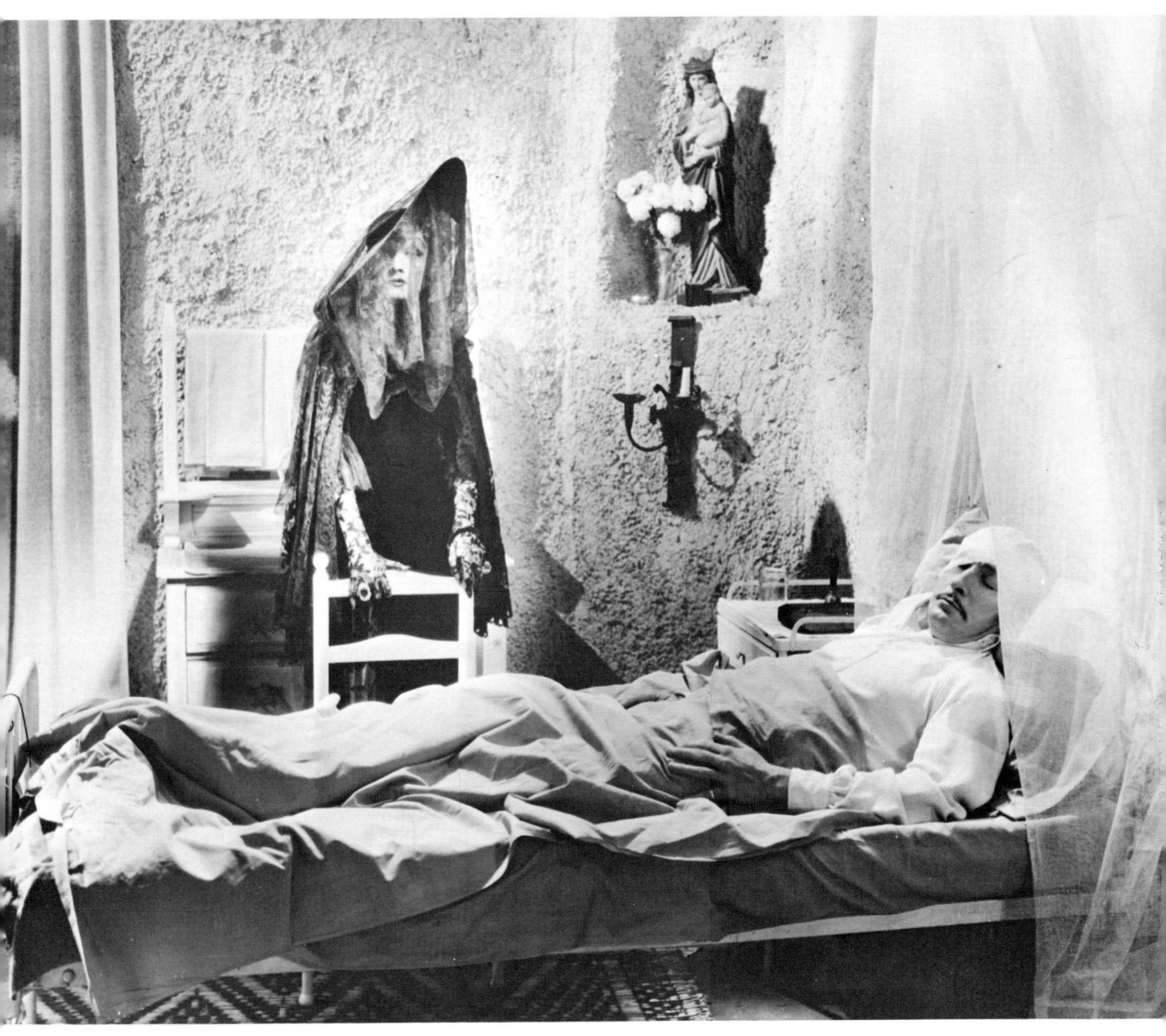

. . . but the experiment went haywire at the film's conclusion, when, swathed in black and grief, she goes to the bedside of the dying Atwill. Did audiences keep straight faces that year?

In considering the septet of von Sternberg/Dietrich films, the variations on a single theme emerge clearly, and the theme is that of a woman leaving one man for another. She leaves Jannings for Albers in *The Blue Angel,* and Menjou for Cooper in *Morocco.* In *Dishonored* she's a combination of both Lola-Lola and Amy Jolly as she gives herself up to save McLaglen. In *Shanghai Express,* she gives herself to Oland to save Brook: it's as if Amy Jolly had not gone off with Tom Brown (Cooper) but instead had waited for him to return, for fate to bring him back to her. Even in *Blonde Venus,* there's another love triangle, with Dietrich leaving Herbert Marshall for Cary Grant, then returning. Finally, in *The Devil Is a Woman,* von Sternberg fulfilled his ultimate fantasy, of having this mysterious, beautiful ideal with him at the deathbed, repentant for ever having left him, forever represented as the Magdalen he named her in *Shanghai Express.*

The poignant element virtually forgotten by historians of Hollywood is that von Sternberg had become the ultimate victim of the myth he had created. Chained to an image of Marlene Dietrich he could only turn this way or that, with kaleidoscopic variations, he had polished her from film to film and transformed her into an almost diaphanous idol. As Mamoulian's *Song of Songs* demonstrated, however, this Galatea could also act — she didn't *need* all that cossetting, all those veils, all that fur — and she just might be able to get along very well, thank you, without her anxious, obsessive, sometimes frightening Pygmalion.

THREE: BATTLE

IN 1935, Ernst Lubitsch, at that time executive in charge of production at Paramount, offered Dietrich a role revealing that some of her versatility had indeed *not* emerged during the von Sternberg years. Lubitsch produced *Desire,* and cast Gary Cooper as her leading man; Frank Borzage was assigned to direct. The story recalls Lubitsch's 1932 classic comedy, *Trouble in Paradise*—lovable jewel thieves, glamorous settings, a beautiful rogue, a dashing accomplice, scintillatingly witty dialogue. Audacious in its comic treatment of amorality, *Desire* indiscriminately equates all kinds of longings: for sex and possessions, for riches and security—but the real emphasis, the real longing, is for La Dietrich. She smiles, beatific and unblinking, right at the men she's double-crossing, and her love scenes with Cooper play perfectly on his image as the *beau idéal* of American manhood in the 1930s: clean, upright (and a little uptight), trusting, a trifle dim but plenty gorgeous. "All you need is a frame and you'd be a masterpiece," he whispers adoringly to her; she could've replied with identical words. Fact is, she's a masterpiece already, and in *Desire* her smiles are beguiling and bemusing. She and Cooper may be the most beautiful couple ever filmed in black and white. Moment to moment, the film seems to say: "Watch this next shot, it's a winner—you'll rarely see faces like this again." We rarely did, or do.

In a Hollywood lounge, she shared a drink with her compatriot, director Fritz Lang, who was then preparing his first American feature. More than a dozen years later, he directed her, but the outcome was less happy than this brief encounter.

"I hated the filming of it," Marlene Dietrich wrote later about her next film, an early Technicolor romance called *The Garden of Allah.* "The ridiculous screenplay . . . everything exasperated

(continued on page 94)

Cecil B. DeMille introduced her and Clark Gable on a segment of the Lux Radio Theatre in 1936. The studio was crammed with photographers, but no one seemed displeased.

Stepping out with Maurice Chevalier and Gary Cooper, 1935. "Men's clothes are so much more comfortable," she said about this time, and that made good copy. The tuxedo must have been a welcome relief from von Sternberg's dizzy excesses.

Ernst Lubitsch produced (and Frank Borzage directed) the glorious Desire *in 1936. Gary Cooper is duped by John Halliday and Dietrich, two accomplished and handsome jewel thieves. Audacious in its comic treatment of amorality, the film indiscriminately equates all kinds of longings: for sex and for possessions, for riches and for security—but the real emphasis, the real longing, is for Marlene.*

A sound and light setup for the stars of Desire. *Dietrich and Cooper were certainly among the most beautiful couples ever rendered in black and white photography.*

The object of Desire, *whether in provocative black . . .*

. . . or challenging white. "All you need is a frame and you'd be a masterpiece," Cooper tells her in Desire.

In The Garden of Allah, *an early Technicolor epic, Charles Boyer portrayed a renegade Trappist monk who illicitly marries an unknowing Dietrich— who has herself gone to the desert to find peace of soul. Way down deep, the film is superficial, and garishly lit. "The ridiculous screenplay exasperated me," Dietrich wrote years later.*

me. But when you're hired to make a film, you have to drink the cup to its dregs even if it's a bad one."

And a bad one it was, although the pain for her must have been somewhat narcotized by the salary of $200,000 which she received from producer David O. Selznick. Based on a Robert Hichens novel, the story concerns a renegade Trappist monk (Charles Boyer) who illicitly marries Dietrich, a woman who has gone to the Moroccan desert to find peace of soul. Neither of them do, of course, until Boyer decides to leave her and return to the monastery. It's not a movie about the search for God: It's simply a variation on the love triangle, and the unseen Presence wins. Besides, Boyer in the film is such a dour prig that only God could endure him for a lifetime commitment. (It's fun to speculate on his monastic brothers' reactions to his return to the cloister . . .)

As the disappointed lady of this impossibly silly film—one which is, when you go way down deep, profoundly superficial—Dietrich proved once again that all she had to do was glance, stand, behold all the silliness around her, and there was cool dignity in the hot desert. Selznick cast her in this sandy love story because of *Morocco*, but she looked overmadeup and overcoiffed here. She was credible in the scenes when she's a confused wife, but her appearance was inappropriate to the setting—not a ringlet disturbed, and the cosmetics just too perfect.

Director Richard Boleslawski had to cope with so much Soul Searching from so many characters in The Garden of Allah *(1936) that the film can't breathe. Here, the dour Boyer again stands apart from everyone — Dietrich, the noble C. Aubrey Smith, the earnest Basil Rathbone. Boleslawski drank tainted water during the shooting of the desert scenes and died shortly afterward.*

What a simple convent schoolgirl wears for a desert retreat: a modest little frock designed by Ernst Dryden for The Garden of Allah . . .

. . . and a chiffon number that producer David O. Selznick had requested, an homage to Dietrich's desert fadeout in Morocco. *This shot, however, is mirage, and to pose for it the actress was in agony with the heat, the wind, the sand.*

Dietrich does not lead the anguished Boyer to do what he does not *want* to do (i.e., confirm his departure from the monastery by marrying her); she simply shows him what he really *does* want—peace of soul, wherever it may take him. At the conclusion, she delivers him, in a closed carriage, to the abbey gates, and the variation on the lonely Dietrich gets a new twist. If she gives all for love, she may have to give him to God, which is of course no competition. Before this finale, however, the audience has to endure a script littered with Hollywood's treacly brand of pseudopiety: "In knowing you and your beauty," Boyer mutters grimly, "I have known God." It's this sort of dimestore aphorism that strikes a blow for atheism in so-called religious movies—and here Selznick ordered director Richard Boleslawski to pile on the invisible angelic choirs, the sweet sententious gestures, the facile resolution and emotional miracle, the starchy nun and oversolemn cleric (in this case, the grandmotherly Lucile Watson and the noble-toned C. Aubrey Smith).

In 1937, Marlene Dietrich applied for American citizenship before Los Angeles County Clerk George Ruperich. She swore allegiance shortly before World War II.

She fared somewhat better in another exotic setting, in Jacques Feyder's direction of James Hilton's *Knight Without Armour,* produced in England by her old friend Alexander Korda in 1937. The melodrama of the first World War, the Russian revolution and a convoluted espionage tale don't much matter here. As a countess, Dietrich (bearing a striking resemblance to Garbo's Anna Karenina) conveys a fineness of spirit deeper than the simple aristocrat she has to portray. There's an innocence and a purity of perception in her love for spy Robert Donat that isn't often evident in her characterizations, and whether dressed in peasant garb and kerchief (for her escape disguise) or in flowing gowns, whether crowned with suds in a (somewhat gratuitous) bath scene or swimming (apparently naked) in a forest paradise, she overcame the tangled material with a performance so deeply felt that it's really the only thing about *Knight Without Armour* that stays in the memory. "I can't sleep," she says at one point, "and I've been trying to pray." That single moment is worth more than all the lush nonsense of *The Garden of Allah.*

By 1937, Marlene Dietrich was the highest paid movie star at work (her compensation was almost $500,000 for *Knight Without Armour*), but she was also one of the most bored, and she leaped at the call from Lubitsch to film *Angel* back at Paramount Studios. Alas, the ordinarily graceful and original Lubitsch (who decided to direct) stumbled with his story of a woman caught between Herbert Marshall (a husband distracted by politics) and Melvyn Douglas, a dashing lover she meets on a Paris holiday. Where the film should have had wit, it offered only starchy poses.

"I never took my career seriously," she said years later about that time. "That doesn't mean that I didn't perform very correctly, that I didn't do my duty. But I was never impressed by my work." She may have been thinking of films like *Angel,* for after its premiere at New York's Radio City Music Hall in November 1937, and a disappointing reaction from critics, Dietrich withdrew to Europe.

Although she had only recently applied for American citizenship (and had again made plain her feelings about Germany — by loudly rejecting at least two offers to return as the queen of Nazi films), Dietrich was sufficiently disappointed by the critics' whin-

In England for much of 1937, Dietrich (here again with an odd resemblance to Greta Garbo) dined with Merle Oberon, Alexander Korda and a clearly worshipful Josef von Sternberg.

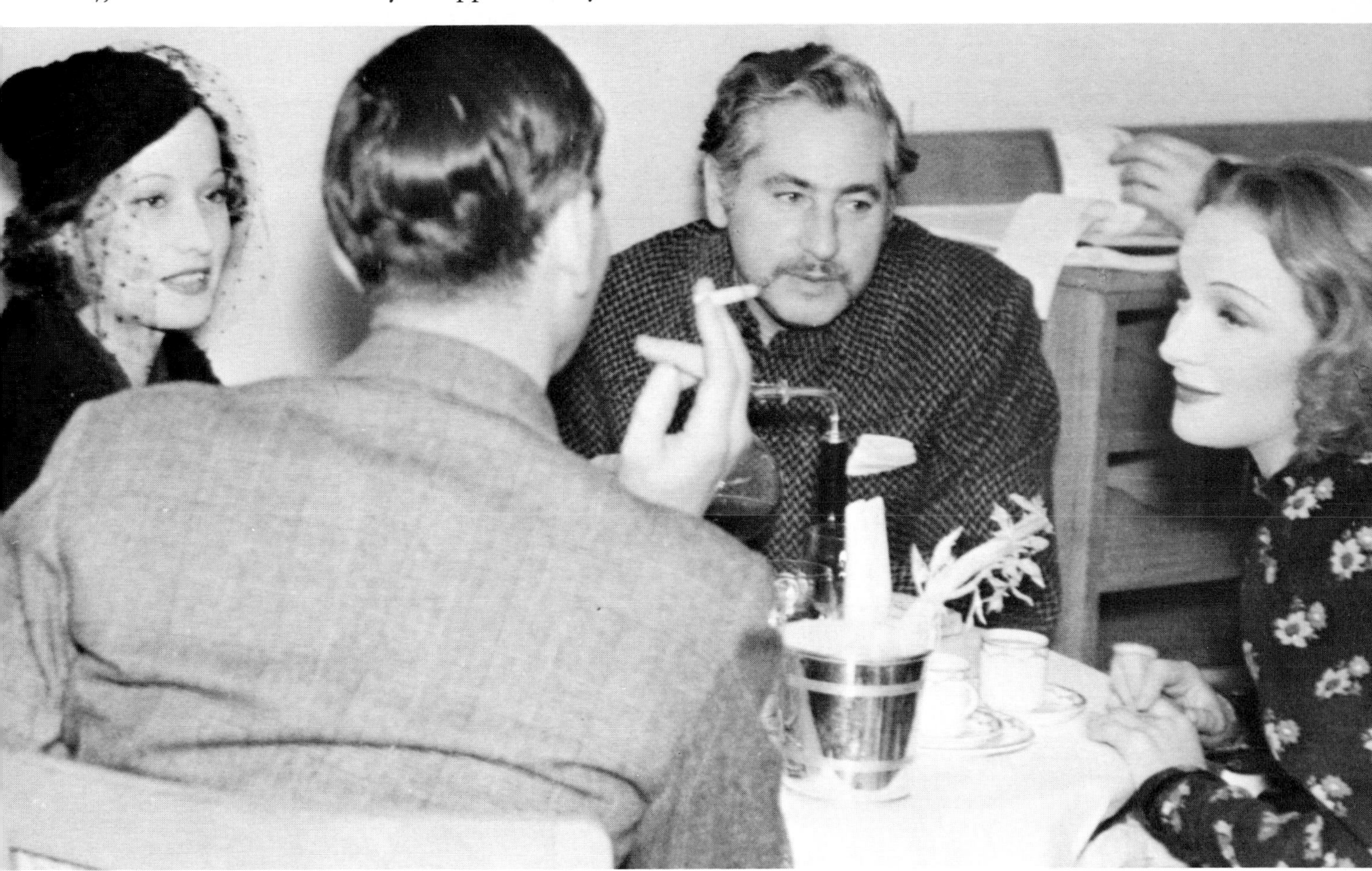

In Jacques Feyder's Knight Without Armour *(1937), Dietrich played a Russian countess very like Garbo's Anna Karenina. The background of World War I, the Russian revolution and a convoluted espionage tale don't matter as much as the simple fineness of spirit with which she invested the character . . .*

. . . whether in moments reflective . . .

. . . or slightly risqué (at least for 1937). The bubble-bath was anachronistic, but what the hell.

Robert Donat was the costar in Knight Without Armour. *Dietrich again seemed to share her strength with her leading man, resulting in perfectly balanced performances that rise above the eminently forgettable narrative. (He does not, however, have the head for this sort of hat.)*

By 1937, Marlene Dietrich was the highest paid working movie actress, but she was also bored to distraction. Ernst Lubitsch's Angel, *for which he and she had great hopes, was a clunky, ungraceful vehicle that substituted narrative starch for the usual Lubitsch wit. After the film's premiere, she withdrew for a protracted European sojourn. Here even* Angel *costar Melvyn Douglas seems unable to cheer her on the Paramount set for the film.*

Producer Joe Pasternak restored Dietrich's popularity with Destry Rides Again *in 1939, and this he did by a violent deglamorization. No longer anything like a Sternbergian mannequin, she's a convincing hellcat as the barroom moll Frenchy. Audiences were caught off guard with this new Marlene, here with James Stewart.*

ing (about *Angel*) to remain away from the United States for almost two years. She visited friends in France and England and rejoined her husband for a Riviera holiday. In the south of France she received an offer from Joe Pasternak, who was then producing pictures for Universal Studios.

Authorized to offer her a mere $75,000, he intended to deglamorize her — to reveal even more facets of her fascination. By early 1939 she was back in Hollywood, working with James Stewart, Brian Donlevy and director George Marshall in the second of four Hollywood versions of the rowdy Western *Destry Rides Again.* In the role of the barroom moll Frenchy, she forever altered her screen image, proved Pasternak right on the mark, and revealed that her talents were indeed richer than many expected.

As a sort of frontier Lola-Lola, Dietrich is heard, then first seen in *Destry Rides Again* singing with a crowd of barroom gunslingers. She totes a six-shooter, cooperates with outlaws and then is amused by the arrival of the quiet, mild deputy (Stewart). Later, kicking and hair-pulling with Una Merkel in the angriest fight of the film, Dietrich shows she's no longer a mannequin. She has more energy than the whole posse, even when she sings the now legendary "See What the Boys in the Back Room Will Have"; she strides and gambles and plays tough — only to reveal, of course, that there's a heart of gold beneath the brassy exterior.

In terms of plot, there's not much for Dietrich to do, and her character doesn't really ring terribly true, but she capitalizes on the broad humor, she looks fetching covered with mud or water, and in her final scene — killed by gunfire as she steps between Stewart and a gun aimed at him — she slides down to her death asking for a last kiss, and wiping the lipstick he had earlier found so overapplied. For just a moment, there's a beacon on a character. Earthy, even vulgar, Dietrich as a barroom moll is still something unpredictable. Amused when others are anxious, serene when they're

The fight scene with Una Merkel in Destry Rides Again *was real enough: the two actresses traded scratches and bruises (all for art's sake, of course) in many takes for director George Marshall. Somehow, even dirt, water, harsh lighting and torn costumes couldn't render Dietrich really* repulsive.

On the set of Destry Rides Again, *Dietrich regularly soaked her aching feet in buckets of ice water while the crew worked out a new camera setup. She was a remarkable trouper, they recalled, enduring all kinds of studio indignities (and this for a salary less than twenty percent of what she had received two years earlier).*

passionate, she simply cannot be contained by the exigencies of a musty Western. And her presence still italicizes — even to the point of sudden death — the ultimacy of love.

Pasternak's gamble with her paid off, and the minds at Universal were sufficiently geared by late 1939 to sign her to a multi-picture contract, with at least two more films to be produced by the benevolent Pasternak. *Seven Sinners,* the first, is an unduly neglected comic masterpiece and one of Dietrich's liveliest, subtlest renderings of a fully tinted personality.

Essentially a burlesque of all the Sadie Thompson epics, the film follows Dietrich as she pursues the American navy all over the South Pacific. Broderick Crawford, Mischa Auer and Albert Dekker literally fall all over each other, the furniture, the pool-tables and the battleships for her sake, and John Wayne (on the brink of stardom the way Gary Cooper and Cary Grant were a decade earlier) diverts Dietrich's attention long enough to add spice to the romantic sugar. There's a subplot about a crook (Oscar Homolka), but nothing matters so much as the elements of real adult humor in *Seven Sinners.* Outrageously bedecked by designer Irene and smoothly directed by Tay Garnett, Dietrich was even more relaxed than in *Destry Rides Again.* Once again, she proved that she was, in some surprising if uncanny way, an actress with a strong sense of irony and a natural gift for timing.

Directed by Garnett from John Meehan's witty script, *Seven Sinners* opens at the Blue Devil Café (clearly an inversion of Dietrich's old hangout in Berlin), and as she sings "I Can't Give You

Seven Sinners *(1940) is a neglected comic gem, and offers one of Dietrich's liveliest, subtlest portraits. Essentially a burlesque of all the Sadie Thompson epics, the film follows her as she follows the American navy all over the South Pacific. Her name is Bijou; her hats were equivalently satirical. Even Willie Fung seems amused.*

Anything But Love" (and then "The Man's in the Navy") we see just how jellified she leaves sailors. Delighting in male attention, she calmly accepts the fact that she's more dangerous than an enemy destroyer. At the billiard table of a doubtful hotel, she learns that American servicemen have arrived. They enter — half a fleet of them, it seems — and stop in a doorway. She turns, takes in this elegant and attractive sea of white-coated men, and whispers

On the brink of stardom, John Wayne was cast opposite Dietrich in Tay Garnett's Seven Sinners. *Earnest, handsome and dull to the point of genius, he seems overwhelmed by her in the film—while she, delighting in male attention, accepts the fact that she's more dangerous than an enemy destroyer.*

"Oh, the navy!" Slowly approaching them, she stops, smiles and asks innocently, "Will someone give me an American . . . [pause] . . . cigarette?"

Of all her films after the von Sternberg era and before 1950, *Desire* and *Seven Sinners* remain perhaps the best, for Dietrich perfected the art of the double-take, the wordless reaction, the slow ingestion of a man's mood and intention. "How about coming to my cabin for a snack?" asks Albert Dekker. She stops cold and stares at him, and he has to elaborate. "A snack is food," he

The reactions are not convincing, and in fact at the end of Seven Sinners *Dietrich and Wayne part: he's too devoted to the navy, and the script suggests something about the sort of patriotism soon to be demanded of many American men.*

continues, and it sounds innocent enough, but Dietrich isn't so sure, and neither are we. *Seven Sinners* continues in vaguely risqué tones, with men fighting in her rooms—fighting so rambunctiously that Wayne gets entwined in her feathery dressing gown, another in one of her hats. "Excuse me," she says lightly, stepping into the room, "I hope I'm not interrupting you girls."

Seven Sinners hops merrily along its satiric way to a quite unexpected seriocomic finale. Dietrich in fact does not find herself in the arms of the powerful, attentive and handsome John Wayne:

he's too devoted a sailor, and the script may have wanted to suggest something about the sort of patriotism that was soon to be demanded of many men. With more than a little courage, Dietrich (called "Bijou" in *Seven Sinners*) slips quietly out of his life, accepts the renewed attention of Albert Dekker (an alcoholic doctor she can change for the better) and suggests that . . . well, life usually goes on with bittersweet compromises like this. She is, at the last, more than a *femme élégante* with a murky history; she's once again the lady with a rich emotional secret or two or three behind her illusion veil.

Dietrich after von Sternberg was a different woman: both lighting and wardrobe conspired to make her look sometimes cheaply ridiculous (as here, with Mischa Auer, in Seven Sinners*), and although her smile always delighted, it was also sometimes (understandably) strained.*

The great French stylist René Clair (left) directed the last of three Dietrich films produced by Joe Pasternak (right): The Flame of New Orleans *(1941) was a period comedy set in old New Orleans; rococo but heavy-handed when it should have been a modest farce, the picture did nothing for the careers of those involved. A party during production provided the happiest moments.*

The last of the Pasternak projects—*The Flame of New Orleans*—was directed by the great French stylist René Clair, who had made *Sous les toits de Paris, Le Million, A Nous la liberté* and (in England) *The Ghost Goes West.* Neither the press nor the public took very warmly to *The Flame of New Orleans,* which has much more of rococo costumes than it has substance or credible humor.

Dietrich is here a woman bent on finding a rich husband (Roland Young is ready to hand), but she falls for the penurious marine roustabout Bruce Cabot, and she dawdles along improbably and not very convincingly disguised as a less refined cousin until all is resolved.

Dietrich tries cannily to challenge the plot's implausibility, however, and she shows how ridiculous men are when they're besotted with a woman. "There's more to being a gentleman than wearing tight pants," she reminds Bruce Cabot in tones apt for a schoolmarm. "And one more piece of free advice: Stay a sailor, sailor—it becomes you more." When she subsequently tries to deceive him, her eyes widen, she smiles triumphantly; her deception, after all, is geared to bringing the man to a deeper understanding of what he *really* wants—the person she *is*, not a counterfeit.

Would the rich Roland Young finally get Dietrich to the altar in The Flame of New Orleans? *Not likely.*

For the next seven years and in as many films, Marlene Dietrich endured one professional disappointment after another. In 1941 she appeared in Raoul Walsh's *Manpower,* as a woman caught between two flinty electric-powermen (Edward G. Robinson and George Raft). The picture is one long buildup to a fight and a catastrophe, and Dietrich was a structural and narrative superfluity—charmingly suave but quite unnecessary—and for all her deadpan sultriness she was misplaced among men for whom romance seems too tame an alternative to tough outdoor work.

She then went from Warner Brothers to Columbia, where director Mitchell Leisen guided her through an amiably bloodless comedy, *The Lady Is Willing.* What the lady was willing to do was adopt an orphaned baby, but Dietrich was clearly not at ease in the film's weepier moments.

Bouncing a baby on those well-exposed knees and gurgling with maternal satisfaction, as she had to do in *The Lady Is Willing,* somehow just didn't seem—well, *sincere.* Which is riotously crazy, since all the evidence points to Marlene Dietrich as the most

In 1941 Hollywood remembered that—oh, yes!—Marlene Dietrich had been famous for her legs. At forty, she happily complied with director Raoul Walsh's wish to spice up a dour melodrama called Manpower. *With suave, deadpan sultriness she coped with an embarrassingly underwritten role . . .*

. . . and in one scene she was at least glad of the chance to do onscreen what she most enjoyed with her family and friends. The stove and the stew are real, the recipe was Marlene's, and late in the day she and the cast tucked into a supper provided by the star.

The only pleasure of Manpower *was working with the amiable and gifted Edward G. Robinson . . .*

. . . and with the admirable and loyal George Raft, who helped her host the "wrap party" at the end of filming Manpower.

Working at Warners and Columbia in the early 1940s, Dietrich was dolled up and lighted to look like any contemporary star. In this unfortunate publicity still, she's not so much Dietrich as Carole Lombard or June Havoc or Lauren Bacall.

Bouncing a baby she wanted to adopt in The Lady Is Willing, *and gurgling with maternal satisfaction, somehow just didn't seem* sincere—*which is curious, since all the evidence points to Marlene Dietrich as the most doting of mothers (and, later, of grandmothers). By 1942, however, her public image was so at variance with the truth that, cast as an attentive parent, she defied credibility.*

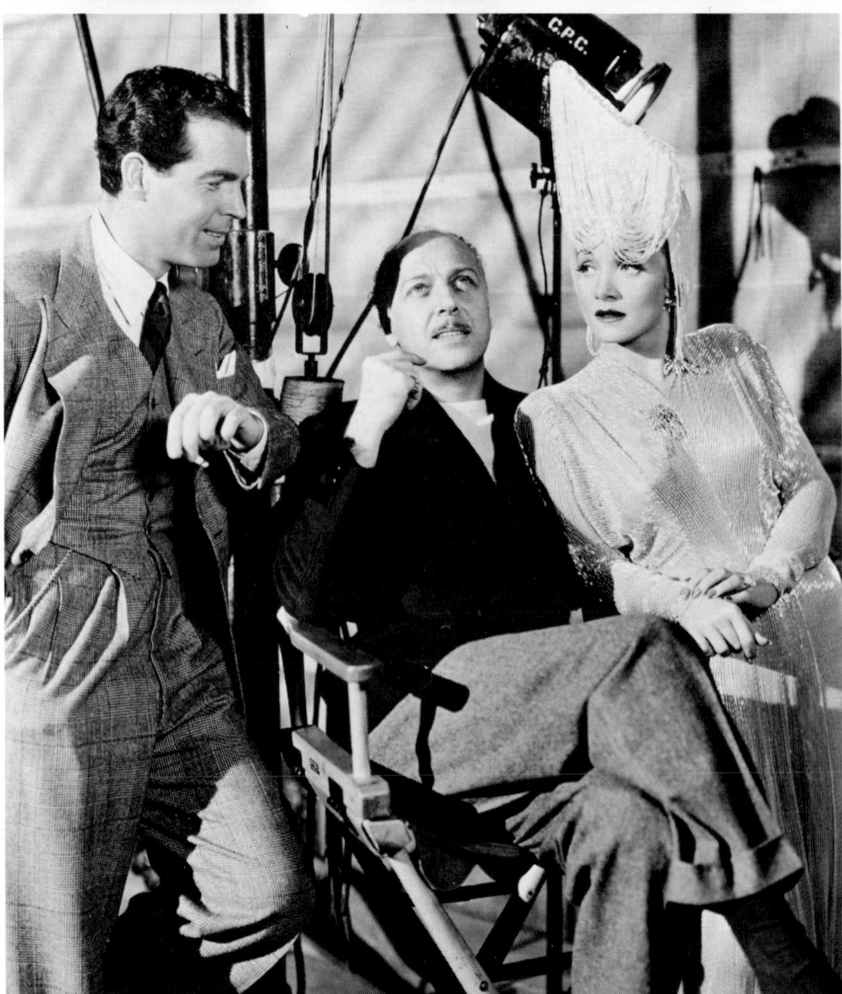

With Fred MacMurray and director Mitchell Leisen on the set of The Lady Is Willing, *1941. Is Leisen dreaming of a different hat design for Dietrich? Almost anything would do.*

The most dramatic moment in the history of The Lady Is Willing *occurred during filming: tripping over a lighting cable, Dietrich took a terrible fall in order to protect the baby she was cradling. The producer offered to shut down the film, but this game lady went on with her duty, broken ankle and clumsy plaster cast notwithstanding. Fred MacMurray might have preferred another view of the famous legs . . .*

. . . and in fact when the cast was removed, as this 1942 publicity still reveals, she was none the worse, and was soon flashing her smile and her legs for Hollywood reporters.

doting of mothers (and, later, of grandmothers), happy in real life to bounce and gurgle over her own or others' offspring.

The most dramatic element in the history of *The Lady Is Willing* occurred during production, in fact: tripping over a lighting cable, Dietrich took a terrific fall in order to protect the baby she was cradling. The producer offered to shut down the film, but our prototypically game lady went on with her duty, a broken ankle and clumsy plaster cast notwithstanding.

This film completed, she went back to the movie-set gin mill, in *The Spoilers,* Ray Enright's directorial contribution to the various versions of Rex Beach's novel about Klondike life circa 1890. As saloon keeper Cherry Malotte (if you can believe that name, you can believe anything), Dietrich is caught between the romantic advances of John Wayne and those of Randolph Scott. The studio apparently hoped to return to the antics of *Destry Rides Again,* but Wayne and Scott are so one-dimensional, and the whole film is so geared to the Great Climactic Fistfight, that Dietrich seems to do little but shift from one lovely leg to the other waiting to see who survives. This time she gets Wayne, who (again!) has a drag scene in Dietrich's ruffly robe.

In Ray Enright's 1942 version of The Spoilers, *Dietrich was returned to a variant of her role in* Destry Rides Again. *This time the setting was the Klondike, circa 1890. Her name was Cherry Malotte, and the boys in the back room crowded round in typical profusion.*

In The Spoilers, *Dietrich was caught between the romantic advances of Randolph Scott and John Wayne who (just as he had appeared in* Seven Sinners*) was bedecked in one of her feathery pieces for one scene.*

Dietrich, Wayne and Scott were teamed to appear together in another picture at Universal — this time a celebration of wartime factories and the people at home who by love and sweat were supporting the war effort. With the unlikely title of *Pittsburgh* on the clapperboard, they threw their personalities into a story of those who rise from smudge-faced miners to tycoons committed to the national interest.

But by 1943 Dietrich was almost stiff with ennui, and she decided to give herself not just onscreen to the struggle against Fascism. Generously and courageously, she entertained American and French troops and helped to encourage and care for men on battle lines in France. Partly inspired by her old love for that country and her new adopted America, and partly by a strong maternal instinct and a horror of war, she saw the young soldiers in battle as those whom she might really help. It was also, apparently, a way of making tangible the gratitude she felt at becoming an American citizen, which occurred in 1939.

Before the tours with the Ninth Army and other fighting branches, and before her visits to the wounded and paralyzed at the end of the war, Dietrich appeared in a cameo for Orson Welles

Also in 1942, the trio from The Spoilers *were reunited in Lewis Seiler's melodrama* Pittsburgh, *a celebration of wartime factories and the people at home who by love and sweat were supporting the war effort. The story was turgid, but these three faces were certainly easy on the eyes.*

and director Eddie Sutherland in *Follow the Boys:* she was sawed in half in a quick magic trick. She also submitted to the ordeal of having her legs painted, the ultimate tastelessness of *Kismet,* in which she writhed and squirmed, apparently uncomfortable with the film and with Ronald Colman's flat chilliness.

When the war ended, she remained in France, to star with her intimate friend and companion, actor Jean Gabin, in a French film called *Martin Roumagnac.* As a high-class prostitute, she's killed by the lovestruck Gabin when he learns about her profession. But neither French nor American audiences (who later saw an absurdly censored version) found much Gallic charm, and Dietrich had to admit another professional disappointment. In late 1946 she was back in Hollywood, more exotic than ever—as a swarthy gypsy wearing *Golden Earrings.* Director Mitchell Leisen guided her again—this time opposite Ray Milland, fresh from his harrowing *Lost Weekend* as an alcoholic for director Billy Wilder. The picture was pure Hollywood hokum, and Dietrich looked dazed. She and Milland were not congenial colleagues, but Dietrich enjoyed working again with Reinhold Schünzel, her costar in 1927 in *The Imaginary Baron.* He had just been directed by Alfred Hitchcock, as had another player in *Golden Earrings* named Ivan Triesault. They were loud in their praise of Hitchcock's film *Notorious,* and they told her that if she ever had the chance to work with Hitchcock she'd be lucky and happy.

For the all-star musical package honoring the many entertainers who gave time to American troops during the war, Dietrich appeared briefly in a magic act with Orson Welles. The film was Eddie Sutherland's Follow the Boys *(1944).*

Dreamily exotic, or pure kitsch? William Dieterle's Kismet *(1944) seemed to treat Dietrich like a Halloween doll. This was the film that sealed her desire to quit Hollywood . . .*

. . . especially after submitting to the ordeal of having her famous legs painted gold for one singularly vulgar musical number.

Generously and courageously, Marlene Dietrich traveled to the centers of war around the world in 1944 and 1945, entertaining soldiers and sailors and ever helping to care for wounded French and American fighting men.

Beginning in June 1944, she made a ten-week tour of North Africa and Italy with the USO Camp Shows. She was, many recalled, the great encourager of everyone.

In Namur, Belgium, in November 1944, she suggested a contest to decide the best legs on soldiers there. Later, she showed them the famous Dietrich legs, effectively winning any contest—and cheering the troops more than ever.

Back in Hollywood briefly in January 1945, she visited the famous Hollywood Canteen almost daily. "In or out of wartime," as the German-American historian Richard Plant characterized her, "Dietrich was essentially a woman who mustered the troops. She was irresistible, and almost everybody adored her—except those who were jealous, or blind."

At battle lines, with the Ninth Army, February 1945, she ignored every discomfort, insisted on the common soldier's diet and clothes, and was a source of endless comfort and pride to the troops.

When Paris was liberated, Marlene Dietrich was—at their insistence—in the French and American entrance march, wearing the medals bestowed on her by two grateful governments.

When the war ended, she remained in France to star with her intimate friend and companion, Jean Gabin, in the French film Martin Roumagnac. *American audiences, later, saw only an absurdly censored version, and not even the French liked it in its complete state.*

As a swarthy gypsy wearing Golden Earrings *for Ray Milland and director Mitchell Leisen (1947), Dietrich found herself in the same kind of hokum she'd endured in* Kismet*—lots of greasepaint and little substance.*

FOUR: LILLI MARLENE

BILLY WILDER — a successful screenwriter in Germany, France and America — had begun directing Hollywood films in the early 1940s. By 1947, his *Double Indemnity* and *The Lost Weekend* were considered remarkable excursions to the dimmer frontiers of human perversity. (*Sunset Boulevard, Some Like It Hot, The Apartment* were yet to come.) As soon as travel to Berlin could be arranged after the war, Wilder visited this broken city to prepare for a film called *A Foreign Affair.* With his typically brilliant, acerbic brand of moral cynicism, Wilder's story criticized the widespread corruption in the military, the black market and the self-righteous treatment of the German people.

For her first appearance in Billy Wilder's controversial postwar satire A Foreign Affair *(1948), a deglamorized Dietrich — playing a former Nazi collaborator — was found brushing her teeth. It's one of her most fully rounded portraits, complex, quietly passionate, full of suppressed fear. With his typically brilliant, acerbic brand of moral cynicism, Wilder's narrative criticized the American occupation of Berlin, the widespread corruption in the military, the black market and the self-righteous treatment given to ordinary Germans by the Allies after the war.*

A supporting character in this seriocomic story was a woman of the theatre who once collaborated with Nazis, was mistress to a highly placed aide to Hitler, and by war's end — living bravely in squalor — had taken an American officer for her lover. From the start, Wilder thought of Marlene Dietrich; she, however, found the idea repellent — until Wilder showed her screen tests by less convincing actresses. Dietrich's professionalism, and her trust in Wilder's personal and aesthetic gifts, overcame her reluctance.

As Erika von Schlütow, Dietrich sang (and was accompanied at the piano by her old friend, composer Frederick Hollander, who had written songs for her since *The Blue Angel*). She took cool stock of the prissy American congresswoman (Jean Arthur) and wrapped the other major characters (played by John Lund and Millard Mitchell) around her strong and generous fingers.

Like Pasternak before him, Wilder understood the value in

During production of A Foreign Affair, *Dietrich entertained cast and crew the way she had entertained family, friends, soldiers and audiences for two decades—with a few numbers on the musical saw. This one happened to belong to a studio carpenter, but she wrested "Falling in Love Again" out of it.*

As the enigmatic Erika von Schlütow in A Foreign Affair, *she took cool stock of the prissy American congresswoman played by Jean Arthur. Nearing fifty, Dietrich seemed a woman light years ahead of winsome little Miss Arthur in understanding human nature. It was just what Billy Wilder wanted.*

deglamorizing Dietrich: Her first appearance in *A Foreign Affair* goes as far in that regard as anyone could expect—hair disheveled, caught in the midst of brushing her teeth, Dietrich is no Amy Jolly, nothing like Concha Perez. But she's not to be taken lightly, not patronized—by an American officer whose support, privileges and devotion she needs, nor by any high-toned moralist.

Erika is an enigmatic character, confident but not really clear, masked with pain and enshrouded in some dark history of betrayal. She sings "Black Market" and "Illusions" and "Ruins of Berlin" with a steely challenge to her cabaret audience, and it's jarring to see Dietrich, in the film-within-the-film, escorted by a Nazi bigwig and introduced to a Hitler look-alike. It's even more astonishing to see her, proud to the end, hauled off by military police to face trial and sentence as a Nazi collaborator. Wilder's unassailable insight, of course, was to see that Dietrich had for twenty years been considered a mysterious woman, and for her role in this film he had to include something that deepened the mystery, that made her presence for the first time credibly suspicious. Critics and audiences complained, however, and not only about Dietrich's role in the picture. They also resented the film's

Masked with psychological pain and enshrouded in some invisible history of betrayal, Dietrich as a woman with a past (in A Foreign Affair*) sang "Black Market" and "Illusions" and "Ruins of Berlin" with a steely challenge to her cabaret audience. She was accompanied onscreen by Frederick Hollander, who had composed songs for her ever since the days of* The Blue Angel.

In January 1948, she met her husband, Rudolf Sieber, at Los Angeles airport when he returned from work in Europe. In spite of decades of estrangement they never divorced, and as this picture shows, they always remained good buddies.

Proud to the moment of her arrest by military police, Erika was played by Dietrich with an uncanny mixture of sassy hauteur *and mysterious wisdom. Here, with Millard Mitchell, she tries to strike a last-minute bargain.* A Foreign Affair *provided her best role in years.*

"Marlene was a professional star," according to Alfred Hitchcock, who directed her in London in 1949 in Stage Fright. *"She was also a professional cameraman, art director, editor, costume designer, hairdresser, makeup woman, composer, producer and director." She was also the only actor whom the benevolently tyrannical Hitchcock allowed substantial creative input on the set.*

exposé of Allied corruption in a blighted city still thought of as enemy territory. *A Foreign Affair* showed Dietrich, nearing fifty, as a woman light years ahead of winsome little Jean Arthur in understanding human nature.

This was exactly the quality Alfred Hitchcock wanted to exploit in his comic thriller *Stage Fright,* made in England during the summer of 1949. (Before beginning work with the formidable if deferential Hitchcock, however, Dietrich appeared in a cameo. As a favor to her friend Mercedes McCambridge and her husband Fletcher Markle, she walked past the camera in Markle's film *Jigsaw.*) Accepting a supporting role for Hitchcock, Dietrich found herself in the curious position of playing a variant on her own image — the role of Charlotte Inwood was part satire on Dietrich's von Sternberg characters, part continuation of those characters.

With Hitchcock there was a strong mutual respect, and a clear understanding on his part about her special knowledge of the technical aspects of the cinema. "Marlene was a professional star," Hitchcock said later. "She was also a professional cameraman, art

As a singing actress of international renown in Stage Fright, *Dietrich plays Charlotte Inwood and sings Cole Porter's suggestive melody "The Laziest Gal in Town." Typically, Hitchcock capitalized on Dietrich's public persona, drawing his audience into the swirling, concentric patterns of the star's puzzling emotional history.*

director, editor, costume designer, hairdresser, makeup woman, composer, producer and director." She was also the only actor to whom Hitchcock allowed substantial creative input on the set: appearing early each day, she astonished the crew and cinematographer Wilkie Cooper by surveying the lighting setups, adjusting an arc here, a shadow or focal length there, ordering a last-minute change of jewelry or hat or makeup. Hitchcock, somewhat disarrayed by this attitude at first, soon saw that her commands actually improved the role and the film; after some early uneasiness they worked matily enough, swapping cigarettes and Hollywood gossip.

As a singing actress of international renown in *Stage Fright*, Dietrich is from her first appearance (in a flashback that turns out to be a lie) breathless with anxiety and with a cunning summoned from moment to moment. The film is a tract on role-playing, a theme dear to Hitchcock's heart: Jane Wyman plays a drama student forced to play a real-life role to solve a crime, no one's identity is ever quite certain, the setting is the theatre, theatre students abound, and no one is more firmly set in the confusion

Appearing early each day on the set of Stage Fright, *Dietrich surveyed the lighting setups, adjusted an arc here, a focal length there, ordered a last-minute change of makeup or hat or jewelry. Hitchcock, somewhat disarrayed by this attitude at first, soon saw that her commands actually improved her role and the film; after some uneasiness they worked matily enough, swapping cigarettes and Hollywood gossip. Here, a light moment during production, with Jane Wyman and Michael Wilding (and Hitchcock facing them).*

With Hector MacGregor and Jane Wyman in Stage Fright, *Dietrich invested a complex role with considerable depth. Playing first a manipulative, then abusive, later frightened and finally sympathetic woman, she seemed to summarize her own cinematic history in this vastly underrated comic thriller.*

No Highway in the Sky *(1951) was a draggy melodrama, an early example of the suspense-disaster variety, but Dietrich was crisply bedecked by Christian Dior in the unfussy, slightly severe early 1950s look. Again, she played a musical comedy star transplanted into a dangerous situation—but always appearing admirably cool.*

than Dietrich's beleaguered, betrayed, bewitching Charlotte Inwood. "Johnny, you do love me, don't you—say that you love me!" she cries in her first moment of dialogue, even before we see her wild eyes. When later we find that this scene was a fabrication by the murderer (who's telling it in flashback to the heroine), it doesn't really matter. Hitchcock, typically, has hooked us into the swirling, concentric patterns of Marlene Dietrich's public image.

"The most glamorous grandmother in the world," the press described her in 1949, and she was still capable of dynamic subtleties. When she sang "The Laziest Gal in Town" (Cole Porter, 1927) in *Stage Fright,* she invested it with more sly, sexy innuendo and more warning than her quietly modulated Edith Piaf homage later in the film ("La Vie en Rose," sung with an almost basso slurriness).

James Stewart, her costar a dozen years before in Destry Rides Again, *returned as the slightly daffy aerophysicist Theodore Honey. Glynis Johns was the flight attendant aboard the suspicious airplane for which there was* No Highway in the Sky.

She returned to England from a postproduction trip to Paris, after discussing with friends there the possibility of a new career —in cabaret. Her next film project, however, was a draggy melodrama. *No Highway in the Sky* was an early example of the suspense-disaster type, with James Stewart as Theodore Honey, an aerophysicist who suspects that an airplane is doomed because of a design flaw. Dietrich, crisply bedecked by Christian Dior in that unfussy, slightly severe early 1950s look, played yet another musical comedy star transplanted into danger. A somewhat damp subplot involving a noble Glynis Johns (as a stewardess) and the widowed Stewart's teenage daughter very nearly sinks the picture, but Dietrich's throaty glamour kept audiences in the theatre and in fact assured the film's profit.

With writer-producer Fletcher Markle, her daughter, Maria, and Maria's husband, William Riva, Dietrich attended opening night of a Judy Garland show at the Palace, New York, October 1951.

Fritz Lang, a compatriot who had also rejected German Nazism and found a professional welcome in America, might have seemed the perfect director for Dietrich. But even Lang—best known for his dark explorations into social and personal pathology *(Dr. Mabuse, Spies, M, Fury)*—had to yield to the prevailing tastes. In 1952, RKO released his production of a confused Western, *Rancho Notorious,* starring Dietrich, Mel Ferrer and Arthur Kennedy.

As Altar Keane, a saloonkeeper who has kept doubtful company with a band of guntoters (Technicolor shades, here, of *Destry Rides Again,* and again and again), Dietrich had little to do other than keep out of the way of the men—which she couldn't seem to do. In what seems a deliberate theft from *Destry,* she's struck down by a bullet intended for another, thus ending a story about the avenging of a murder. Bored with herself and everyone round her, Altar Keane should have been the perfect role for Dietrich; she's even given lines apposite to her legend, like "Every year is a threat to a woman." But her color makeup was garish, her costars were wooden and her character was underwritten.

The press, as always, detailed her virtues. Lang, with whom she barely spoke by the end of production, did not. And with *Rancho Notorious* and its Technicolored muddle, Marlene Dietrich turned her back on Hollywood.

But not on performing, nor on pleasing millions. For several years in the 1950s, she worked hard at polishing a cabaret act, singing, chatting from the stage with audiences in America and Europe, and alternating these travels with frequent turns at radio melodrama. Her most enjoyable occupation, however, was that of grandmother to Maria's children. By this time Dietrich had redecorated her Park Avenue apartment (not a palatial residence at all, but given scope and splendor by a profusion of mirrors). Here the children could often be found, and residents of New York's Upper East Side recall Dietrich pushing their strollers, buying ice cream in Central Park, taking the children to the zoo and to playgrounds. No white-capped, hired nanny for *her* grandchildren.

Grandma's life was interrupted in 1956, however, when she was lured by the flashy producer Mike Todd for a cameo in the epic *Around the World In Eighty Days*—again, as a vintage San Francisco saloonkeeper. This time the boys in the back room were Frank Sinatra and the story's peripatetic David Niven and Cantinflas. Dietrich's plantinum-white wig and scarlet Victorian minigown lit up her few seconds of screen time, and her cheerful face and lithe figure gave the lie to *Rancho Notorious:* The years had been no threat at all to this woman.

As Altar Keane, a saloonkeeper who has kept doubtful company with a band of guntoters in Fritz Lang's Rancho Notorious *(1952), Dietrich summoned shades of* Destry Rides Again. *It should have been a better role, but the character was underwritten and her collaboration with Lang full of tension.*

She took Rancho Notorious *in good humor, however, and even had the sport to appear in this very nearly parodic publicity still for the film, complete with butterfly at a crucial spot.*

Her costars in the Lang film were Arthur Kennedy and Mel Ferrer—one too decent and the other too chic to be credible—and at the end, in a deliberate recall from Destry Rides Again, *she's struck down by a bullet intended for another. Pity; it should have hit the script-book, much earlier.*

In 1951, "the world's most glamorous grandmother" (thus the press) and her daughter Maria, celebrated twenty-one years in America.

Grandma's quiet family life for much of the 1950s was interrupted in 1956, when she was hired by producer Mike Todd for a cameo in the epic Around the World in Eighty Days*—again, to play a vintage San Francisco saloonkeeper. The boys in the back room this time were Cantinflas, David Niven and Frank Sinatra. Her platinum wig and scarlet Victorian minigown were as bright as her smile.*

As she moved gracefully and decorously toward her late fifties, Marlene Dietrich grew more and more unhappy with the kind of roles she was offered. When the Italian director and former matinee idol Vittorio De Sica invited her to the Riviera to costar in *The Monte Carlo Story,* she accepted at once. She had loved De Sica's contributions to cinema as the director of deeply felt, profoundly humane neorealist classics (*Shoeshine, The Bicycle Thief, Umberto D., The Roof*). As a still dashingly handsome actor he charmed her and everyone else in the production.

De Sica played a member of faded royalty addicted to Monte Carlo's gambling tables. To support himself and his pastimes, he decides to marry a rich woman (Dietrich) who—as in *Trouble in*

When the Italian director and former matinee idol Vittorio De Sica invited Dietrich to the Riviera in 1957 to costar in The Monte Carlo Story *for director Samuel A. Taylor, she accepted. The film was a disaster except for this handsome pair . . .*

Paradise and *Desire*—turns out to be an elegant and amusing fraud with her own designs on his dwindling fortune, and who is actually poorer than he.

The film is awkward, devoid of feeling and spontaneity, mostly because the dialogue was dubbed later and everything seems sufficiently "off" to make the characters appear as if they're all moving on command. Decked out in primal colors by designer Jean Louis, Dietrich moves carefully, but in only one scene do you believe she's really enjoying herself—when she insists on taking over De Sica's kitchen.

. . . and Jean Louis's elegant wardrobe for her.

In September 1958, her good friend Noël Coward escorted her to a ballet opening in New York. Their friendship spanned three decades, until his death in 1973.

Billy Wilder gave Dietrich the complex role of Christine Vole in his film of Agatha Christie's Witness for the Prosecution *(1958). She gave the finest performance of her film career as a woman with more layers than onion skin. Here, in an early flashback, she summarized nothing so much as early Dietrich, in the cabaret singing of "I May Never Go Home Anymore."*

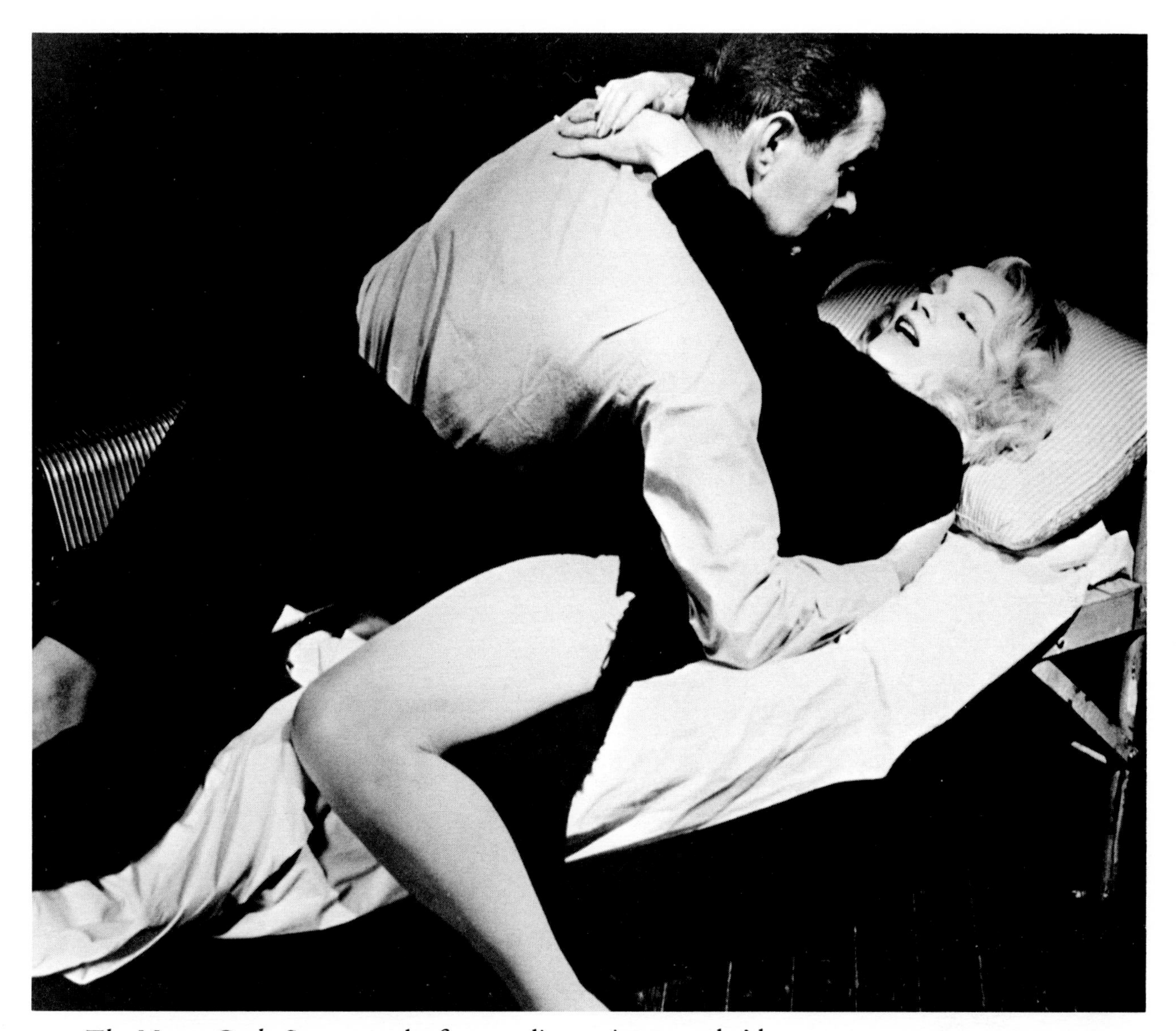

This shot (with Tyrone Power) never appears in Witness for the Prosecution—*it's much less leggy in the finished film, where the two are never so intimate. But lobby stills, for publicity, often promise more than the film delivers.*

The Monte Carlo Story was the fiercest disappointment she'd known in years, and the time could not have been more auspicious for her call from Billy Wilder. He was preparing to film Agatha Christie's successful play *Witness for the Prosecution,* and he suggested that she play the lead. Familiar with the role and the text, Dietrich accepted and returned to America from a long sojourn in Paris. She was about to render the finest film performance of her career, and a kind of summary of what she'd represented on screen for the previous three decades.

That it was her most complex and demanding role never fazed her for a moment. She played Christine Vole, a former actress, brought from Germany to England after the war by soldier Tyrone Power. In the complicated plot, she schemes to prove to judge and jury that she is untrustworthy as a witness against her husband, who is accused of murdering a woman for money. As she hopes, the jury believes her husband innocent, that he has been framed by

Charles Laughton, too, gave a splendid performance in Witness for the Prosecution, *as a crusty attorney. His relationship with Dietrich in the story was never so genial as this candid, at a rehearsal, suggests.*

her—but he is indeed guilty, and she has risked everything for him. When she greets him on his release from the trial, she finds that he's eagerly awaited by another woman. Scorned, she kills him on the spot, and at the finale attorney Charles Laughton, who had successfully pleaded the innocence of the guilty man, now agrees to defend Dietrich.

As a woman who plots and perjures herself for love and who finally kills for love spurned, Dietrich gave herself fully and with complete credibility to the twists of character and of plot. Working closely with Wilder and cinematographer Russell Harlan, she was presented simply, framed neatly, unadorned and unflattered by most of the tricks of the trade. But of course Marlene Dietrich's plainness is never less than breathtaking.

Before her first appearance in the film, Laughton warns an associate about her character: "Bear in mind she's a foreigner, so be prepared for hysterics or even a fainting spell. Have smelling salts ready."

Suddenly Dietrich's voice is heard off-camera: "I don't think that will be necessary."

Only then do we see her, framed in a doorway, a slightly remote figure in a tailored suit, slouch hat and gloves. In utter simplicity, photographed full-face, she is no goddess, but a defiant archetype of Woman. "I never faint, because I'm not sure that I will fall gracefully," she says unblinkingly as she and the camera move slowly toward each other like lovers, "and I never use smelling salts because they puff up the eyes." The dialogue seemed created for none other than Marlene Dietrich.

The requisite song ("I May Never Go Home Anymore") is in fact more than just a requisite song: in an extended flashback told by Tyrone Power, we see Dietrich as she's supposed to have been several years earlier, in a cabaret very like the Blue Angel. Sporting a sailor's suit, accompanying herself on the accordion and wearing a shockingly cheap blond wig, she of course causes mayhem, and when her trouser leg is torn in a melee, well, it's only what's expected when a woman like this is on the scene. It's a measure of Dietrich's composure, her unstudied confidence at this stage of her life and career, that the role of Christine Vole revealed several conflicting facets of character. Her eyes alive with pretense and passion, her mouth defiant against age—against everything except betrayal—Dietrich immersed herself in the role, poured a wholeness of feeling into hysterical scenes and, more than a generation later, astonishes film students who may momentarily have the wrong idea that she was just another legendary face in the history of the movies.

Moments later, before the camera, the famous enigmatic gaze and quiet demeanor prevailed. "All you have to do with Dietrich," according to director Billy Wilder, "is to frame her properly. Her presence takes care of everything else."

Her eyes are alive with passion, her sense of irony is craftily controlled. Dietrich wears only plain suits in Witness for the Prosecution: *all the glamour has been harnessed to a stinging portrait of a remarkably loyal woman willing to perjure herself for love . . .*

. . . and whose confidence is devastated at last by the betrayal of that love.

Tea-time at the studio during the elaborate rehearsals for Witness for the Prosecution: *Dietrich with Laughton, Power and Wilder.*

Of her other performance in 1958—a cameo as a darkly erotic madame in a Mexican bordello, dispensing advice to Orson Welles in his fascinating film *Touch of Evil*—Dietrich remained forever enthusiastic: "I was never better in my life than I was for Orson in that teensy part," she said frequently afterward. Some admirers might agree, although the character as written is dangerously close to what Susan Sontag called camp. "Lay off the candy bars," she counsels the enormous Welles, matching him cigar for cigar.

Her last important motion picture was Stanley Kramer's long and turgid *Judgment at Nuremberg,* a courtroom drama about the trial of the Nazi war criminals. As Frau Bertholt, the widow of a German officer, she tries to explain to Spencer Tracy, the presiding American judge at Nuremberg: "I have a mission—to convince you that we [Germans] are not all monsters."

A weary, slightly arrogant aristocrat, Dietrich gave the star-studded motion picture a calm confidence, even though her brows were for some scenes drawn so high she seems in a perpetual state of lethal surprise. For her first appearance this time, she was photographed in a kitchen; well dressed, she quietly fetches groceries to take to her own humble flat, since the house she and her husband owned is now for Tracy and his official staff. Her face is not quite a blank, but there is a kind of Berlin Wall around her, a cool mask she never really puts aside in *Judgment at Nuremberg.* This is a quietly nervous performance, her eyes shifting left and right even when she and Tracy stroll through a dark street, the measures of "Lilli Marlene" heard off-camera, a song to which she finally yields and sings a few phrases.

As Frau Bertholt, the widow of a German World War II officer, Dietrich tries to explain to Spencer Tracy (presiding judge at the Nuremberg war trials), "I have a mission—to convince you that we [Germans] are not all monsters." She gave a quietly nervous performance in Judgment at Nuremberg *(1961), her face a cool mask of withdrawal. "I'm not fragile," she tells him. "I'm a daughter of the military. It means I was taught discipline." She could have been speaking about Marlene Dietrich.*

Cast and crew of Judgment at Nuremberg *found Dietrich nothing like the role she took in the picture. Gregarious, warm, helpful, fun-loving, she was, as usual, appreciated by all who worked with her.*

"I'm not fragile," she says to Tracy later. "I'm a daughter of the military. It means I was taught discipline." And with these curiously autobiographical remarks Dietrich seems to have rung down the curtain on her film career. The character of Frau Bertholt, insisting that despite atrocities people must move on, no longer hating, is not fully explored. But at the end, when Tracy rings to bid farewell, she sits in shadow near the telephone, leaving his call unanswered. Her anguish is palpable, though a strange aloofness hangs over her performance, rather as if this proud lady has abandoned hope of the world's maturity. Her compassion is unsentimental, her share in the world's incompleteness is felt and acknowledged. Everything, finally, fades but for a little wisdom and a little caring. Marked and sealed with more experience than we'll ever know she had, her features at the end of *Judgment at Nuremberg* are a testimony forever captured, always available to us. Noble? Yes, but more: recognizably human and frail and therefore eternally lovable, eternally mysterious.

*Dietrich's penultimate screen appearance: she steps from a limousine to the House of Dior, a momentary apparition in white for an Audrey Hepburn film (*Paris When It Sizzles*, 1964).*

In the 1960s, composer Burt Bacharach was conductor, arranger, friend, guide, guardian angel for a series of Marlene Dietrich appearances "in concert" around the world. She justified for modern audiences the feeling that Shakespeare's words about Cleopatra could be applied to her:

"Age cannot wither her, nor custom stale
Her infinite variety."

Marked and sealed with experience, her features are a testimony forever captured, always available to us. Noble? Yes, but more: recognizably human and frail, and therefore eternally mysterious.

ACKNOWLEDGMENTS

I AM GRATEFUL to Michelle Snapes, of the British Film Institute Film Stills Library, and to Mary Corliss, of the Museum of Modern Art's Film Stills Library, for their kind assistance in locating rare photographs that appear in this book. In various other ways, I was graciously aided during the course of this project by Joseph Kennedy, Michael Mattil, Colleen Mohyde and Richard Plant. Gregory Young sat patiently and attentively when I read paragraphs aloud; I am grateful for his constancy. Once again, William Phillips has been a perceptive editor and a devoted friend. I have dedicated the book to Elaine Markson, my literary agent. Her affection and encouragement redeem the meaning of professional representation.

D.S.
February 9, 1985

SELECTED BIBLIOGRAPHY

BAXTER, PETER, ed. *Sternberg.* London: British Film Institute, 1980.

DE NAVACELLE, THIERRY. *Sublime Marlene.* London: Sidgwick & Jackson, 1984.

DICKENS, HOMER. *The Films of Marlene Dietrich.* Secaucus: Citadel, 1968.

DIETRICH, MARLENE. *Marlène D.* Paris: Grasset, 1984. (This is a translation into French by Boris Matthews and Francoise Ducout, based on an unpublished manuscript in English.)

HIGHAM, CHARLES. *Marlene: The Life of Marlene Dietrich.* New York: Norton, 1977.

SARRIS, ANDREW. *The Films of Josef von Sternberg.* New York: The Museum of Modern Art/Doubleday, 1966.

SILVER, CHARLES. *Marlene Dietrich.* New York: Pyramid, 1974.

VON STERNBERG, JOSEF. *Fun in a Chinese Laundry.* New York: Macmillan, 1965.

WALKER, ALEXANDER. *Dietrich.* New York: Harper & Row, 1984.

WEINBERG, HERMAN G. *Josef von Sternberg.* New York: Dutton, 1967.

Photographs on the following pages courtesy of *The British Film Institute:* ii, 4, 7, 11, 12, 15, 16, 20–22, 25, 27, 32, 33, 35, 37, 40, 43, 44, 47–51, 54–56, 60, 62, 63, 66, 67, 69 (right), 70, 72 (left), 73, 74, 75 (top), 76–80, 83 (top), 84, 90, 91, 93, 94, 96–107, 109, 110, 113, 114 (bottom), 116, 117 (right), 118, 119, 120 (top), 121 (left), 125, 126, 130 (right), 131 (bottom left), 132–135, 138 (left and top right), 139, 141 (left), 142, 143, 145, 146, 149, 152

Courtesy of the *Museum of Modern Art:* 13, 17, 18, 23, 30, 34, 38, 39, 41, 42, 45, 46, 52, 53, 58, 61 (right), 64, 65, 68, 71, 72 (right), 75 (bottom), 81, 82, 83 (bottom), 85, 88, 92, 111, 112, 114 (top), 117 (left), 120 (bottom), 121 (right), 122–124, 128, 130 (left), 131 (top left and right), 136, 138 (bottom right), 140, 141 (right), 144, 148, 151

This book was designed and paged by Mike Fender of Cambridge, Massachusetts. It was set in 12/15 and 9/11 Sabon *by Progessive Typographers of York, Pennsylvania, with headlines in Letraset* Papyrus *provided by the designer. It was printed on 80 pound* Patina *by Maple-Vail of Binghamton, N.Y. and bound in Joanna Arrestox B by Maple-Vail.*